A GUIDE TO
MUDLARKING
ON THE RIVER
THAMES

A GUIDE TO MUDLARKING ON THE RIVER THAMES

HUNTING FOR TREASURE

EMMYLOU VAXBY

First published in Great Britain in 2026 by
Fonthill
An imprint of
Pen & Sword Books Ltd
Yorkshire – Philadelphia

ISBN 978-1-03614-701-3

A CIP catalogue record for this book
is available from the British Library.

Typeset in SabonLTStd 10/13 by
SJmagic DESIGN SERVICES, India.
Printed and bound in India by Replika Press Pvt. Ltd

The Publisher's authorised representative in the EU for product
safety is Authorised Rep Compliance Ltd., Ground Floor,
71 Lower Baggot Street, Dublin D02 P593, Ireland.
www.arccompliance.com

For a complete list of Pen & Sword titles please contact

PEN & SWORD BOOKS LIMITED
George House, Units 12 & 13, Beevor Street, Off Pontefract Road,
Barnsley, South Yorkshire, S71 1HN, England
E-mail: enquiries@pen-and-sword.co.uk
Website: www.pen-and-sword.co.uk

or

PEN AND SWORD BOOKS
1950 Lawrence Rd, Havertown, PA 19083, USA
E-mail: uspen-and-sword@casematepublishers.com
Website: www.penandswordbooks.com

To my grandfathers.

Foreword

When Emmylou approached me to write the foreword to her book, I was extremely honoured and excited to do so. The passion that Emmylou has for mudlarking and discovering long-forgotten treasures from the past in the River Thames jumps out from each page. Her vibrant way of writing reminds me of how I too felt as a child when I was filled with wonder at the natural world around me. For me it started when I searched for natural treasures in my garden on our small farm in Cornwall. There I became lost in my own world, as I observed insects, collected empty snail shells, studied fungi and seed pods and marvelled at the intricacy of it all. I also spent hours on the beach collecting shells, pebbles and pieces of seaworn glass to make art. When I moved to London in the late 1990s, the Thames foreshore at Greenwich became a replacement beach for the Cornish beaches I missed from my childhood.

I still remember the very day I was walking along the foreshore at low tide in Greenwich over twenty years ago when I discovered a small portal into the past! I looked down and spotted a coin nestled among the rocks. I reached down to pick it up thinking it was a modern coin but then I realised it was a George III coin from 1799. As I held it in my hand, I was struck with the realisation that

I was the first person to hold it since the eighteenth century and I wondered who might have dropped it all those years ago. It really got my imagination going and from that day there was no going back. I acquired my mudlarking permit from the Port of London Authority and I returned to the foreshore as often as I could.

Many years later mudlarking is a huge part of my life and I continue to be passionate about researching the history behind the objects I find in the mud of the Thames. In particular, telling the stories of long-forgotten people from the past is something I feel compelled to do and it is through my mudlarking finds that I am able to do this. An early nineteenth-century pewter tankard with a name engraved on it, a seventeenth-century trader's token, an iron barge padlock, these are just some of the objects which have led me to discover people who lived, worked or passed through London many years ago. My favourite find is not what many people would expect and goes to show that not all treasures are gold and silver. A humble brass luggage tag bearing the name of a man who fought in the First World War and who I then discovered was buried in a pauper's grave close to where I live, is for me the essence of mudlarking and is the kind of treasure that I am seeking when I put on my boots and head down to the river at low tide.

The joy I experience while mudlarking is enhanced many times over by being able to share it with a wide audience around the world through my YouTube channel. I have seen how it appeals to young and old alike but it is particularly special to see and hear from children who are inspired by the magic of mudlarking. This is how I met Emmylou, who came with her family to see a talk I gave during the Totally Thames Festival in London in 2021. I was struck immediately by Emmylou's sense of curiosity about the artefacts I spoke about that day and her determination to learn more.

Four years after meeting Emmylou I can see that she has lost none of her enthusiasm for the art of mudlarking. She has learned so much about the River Thames and the history contained in it. Remarkably, her dedication and enthusiasm have led to her writing a book on the subject. I believe Emmylou's story will inspire and spark the imagination of a future generation of mudlarks and encourage young readers to venture outside, to look closely, to wonder about the past and maybe even try mudlarking for themselves.

I also have great admiration for the way that Emmylou has combined her passion for the history in the Thames with her obvious love and care for the environment. The way she addresses the important topic of plastic pollution is a huge inspiration. A couple of years ago she invited me to join her and her friends for a river clean up, as part of Wapping's Plastic Free Community, an organisation she founded and which carries out regular foreshore clean ups. It's important voices such as Emmylou's that will encourage other youngsters to respect and care for our rivers so that generations to come will be able to find the same solace and pleasure in life enhancing river side activities as we do today.

I am incredibly proud of Emmylou for writing this book. It's a wonderful achievement. I hope that as you read it, you will be drawn in to feel the same spark of excitement that she felt, and that I felt all those years ago on my first trip to the Thames foreshore.

Nicola White
London
October 2025

Emmylou Vaxby and Nicola White. (*C. Kontz*)

A large barge on the Thames photographed from Stepney Beach. (*E. Vaxby*)

Preface

The start to my story

I walked with my friend to the stone steps. Her mum followed close behind, with Pascual the dog sniffing at things like dogs do. I weaved through the metal bars, protecting anything with wheels from sliding down the steps. As I placed my rubber boot upon the cold cobbles, I felt the moss sink beneath my feet. The songs of water birds and the sounds of the sea were within arm's reach. I could feel it in my bones. As we entered the foreshore, bowing under the small wooden bridge above us, I felt like I had been transported to somewhere else, to a different time. Surely this was not London anymore: the squelch of the mud, the rustle of the fragile pieces of pottery were all carried by the summer breeze. It felt like a different world to the London I knew—the one with traffic, noise and busy people.

A boat ran past, breaking the trance. Pascual started barking at the vessel. I could see famous London landmarks dotting the banks opposite me: the tall towers in Canary Wharf and the Thames starting to meander. Tower Bridge was also hovering over the Thames in the distance. The river didn't feel so big anymore with the huge walls that lined the edge of the pebble beach towering over you.

Then I looked down, and saw a mosaic floor. Pieces of pottery and stone, puzzled together to make the ground I was standing on. The sight of all of these tiny treasures was overwhelming, but in the best way possible! I slowly bent down and picked up a piece of glass, wet from the tide. I held it up to the sun, which was shining down onto the water making the river sparkle like a thousand blue diamonds. The piece of glass cast a beautiful aqua colour onto my small, fragile fingers. I placed the gem into my little bag which was decorated with a strawberry pattern. I carried on looking for glass, presuming that was the only secret these shores had for me. But, I was wrong. My friend's mum had a licence, she knew all about what we could find. She pointed out a piece of pottery to us. It had been lying there in plain sight! I must have seen it a hundred times while I was scanning the floor. I inspected what she had shown me. The ceramic didn't have rough edges, they were smooth and soft. The pottery had blue paint on it, like the ones my grandmother brings us when we eat dessert.

I'm not sure how long we stayed by the river, but it must have been a while because the sun had moved. My little bag was getting heavy, filled with patterned pottery and shards of broken glass. Almost bursting at the seams; when I looked inside, it looked like a rainbow had exploded! There were blues and greens in the glass and reds and yellows dancing on the pottery. There were also bits of cream pipe stems, sprinkled in the mass of things I had found.

Another boat went past. This time much faster! It was like a rocket, zooming through London. It created astronomic waves, crashing down onto the pebbles: I was worried I'd be washed away! I thought the murky water looked a lot like chocolate milk, but I knew I probably shouldn't drink it…

By now my yellow gum boots were covered in mud, my fingers were a little cold from the breeze that swept between the water droplets upon my fingertips. My friend had found some pottery that looked like it would perfectly fit mine! It was like magic: the two corners perfectly slid into one another, completing the puzzle.

Above: A family of swans onlooking the Thames at Stepney Beach near Limehouse. The buildings of Canary Wharf can be seen in the background. (*E. Vaxby*)

Right: A view onto the Thames from the foreshore. (*E. Vaxby*)

We had been mudlarking in the same spot, so these fragments of history had probably broken just before we came down the slippery steps, but that didn't stop these 5-year-olds from getting very excited! We might not have found any buried treasure, but these broken pieces of pottery, chipped on the edges, would forever hold value in our hearts.

This all happened somewhere between Wapping and Limehouse, on the foreshore of the Thames many moons ago. Little did I know that mudlarking would not only become a hobby and great passion, but I would write a whole book about it! I have now been mudlarking quite regularly for years, and my collection has grown to hundreds of treasures. This adventure I have been describing was my first time mudlarking, and I went with my best friend and her mum. I didn't have any background knowledge when I went, just that what we would find was probably very, very old. I came home with a bag packed with glass and pottery and a couple of oyster shells too. They had glinted in the sunlight and their iridescence caught my eye. I still remember that day, though it is a little hazy. However, the treasures sit safely, in a little bag covered in strawberries at home.

Contents

PART I

IN THE MUD

1

What is Mudlarking?

Let me introduce you to the world of mudlarking.

Mudlarking has been around for hundreds of years. It first became popular in the eighteenth and nineteenth centuries, when there was a very large gap between the lower and upper classes. The rich had it easy, while the poor had to find ways to make a living. People born into wealthy households had the finest education and didn't have to do very laborious jobs. Those not as fortunate would work for people higher in the social hierarchy, whether they were servants, chimney sweepers or making things in factories. The rich looked down on those with less than them, and didn't let people from lower classes move up in life. Marrying beneath you was seriously looked down on and seen as a 'last resort'.

So, what was it like on the foreshore during the times of the Georgians and Queen Victoria? Trade from across the British Empire would come into the port of London and the docks in the East; bringing spices, silk, wool, rice, tobacco and building materials such as timber. The river was busy with ships going in and out of London and shouts from sailors filled the air. People were hurrying across bridges to bustling markets where some of the fresh fruits and vegetables from the boats were being sold. The smell of fresh fruits and vegetables mingling with the rotten, fallen ones was grasped by the wind, accompanied by the stink of fish and fresh meat. These markets served the working class, providing necessities like food and also items like clothes.

The Thames has seen all kinds of boats: wherries, hoys, cutters and barges. Some ships in history would end up sinking and their goods forever lost to the river ... *unless we find them*! Evidence of the old shipping industry is still in the street and warehouse names—like Cinnamon Street and Tobacco Dock by the old wharfs in Wapping (an area in East London nestled just below Shadwell and Whitechapel). Ropemaker's Fields, Sailmaker's House to name a few more places linked to the river. Limehouse, Rotherhithe—also known as Redriff in the past—and Shadwell were all places the ships would dock. We can now see the redeveloped busy shipping quarter: warehouses and wharfs with cranes that have been transformed into apartment houses. While on the river, clippers and speed boats race up and down the inner-city and yachts and houseboats still live in little harbours, like St Katherine's Docks.

London was even known as the 'warehouse of the world'. Some of these wharves still carry the name they were originally given, describing where the cargo was coming from like Canary Wharf (from the Canary Islands), West India Quay (the West Indies) and East India Dock (which closed in 1967).

The first thing you see when coming back up from the foreshore in Wapping are rows of these old warehouses, towering over the narrow-cobbled streets. There used to be many more taverns and inns but these have been replaced with cosy cafes and supermarkets. However, the oldest riverside pub is still there: The Prospect of Whitby. The pub has been standing since around 1520, originally named The Pelican. The stairs to the right are called Pelican Stairs but I am not sure why—I haven't ever seen a pelican there! For a while it was also referred to as The Devil's Tavern, as the place was frequently visited by thieves and smugglers. They also say that Charles Dickens and Samuel Pepys were among some famous customers. Behind this historic place is one of my favourite mudlarking spots. There is a noose outside standing on the foreshore, showing where the old Execution Dock lay.

Above: A small boat near the foreshore in Wapping, with a larger boat and Canary Wharf in the background. (*E. Vaxby*)

Below: Lots of boats by Wapping. (*E. Vaxby*)

Right: A view of The Prospect of Whitby pub from the street. (*E. Vaxby*)

Below: On the foreshore by Limehouse with an interviewer, with Canary Wharf in the distance. (*E. Vaxby*)

The London Docks were still in use up until 1969 when the sailing ships were replaced by larger container ships which could not fit in the docks, and the port moved out of the heart of London. The modern port of London now reaches from Teddington in the west to the start of the North Sea in the east and is controlled by the Port of London Authority, also known as the PLA, which was founded on 31 March 1909. They are the ones giving permits to today's mudlarks, but no licences were needed in Victorian times. By the 1930s the docks and this port gave jobs to over 100,000 people! This number declined after most of the docks closed between the 1960s and the 1980s. For example, the West India Dock closed in 1980. They were not cut out to accommodate the larger vessels that were now being used, and container ships could easily be unloaded onto trucks without the need to store things in warehouses before distribution. Before the PLA, people would have let themselves down onto the foreshore. There was, however, the Thames River Police, established in 1798 and initially based in Wapping. They prevented theft from ships as those boats were often found with some cargo stolen.

The East End was a rough and dangerous place back then! There were robberies, murders and just a general uneasy atmosphere. In 1701, Captain Kidd the Scottish privateer was hanged in Wapping. Nowadays this side of London is calm and quiet, but hints of the past still shine through. The Wapping Hockey Club is called the Wapping Kidds, just like the old captain. The Thames River Police eventually merged with the Metropolitan Police, evolving into the Marine Policing Unit. Their base is still in Wapping too.

Wapping—one of my favourite mudlarking spots—has been at the heart of the port for centuries. It was the settlement of Waeppa's people and, at some point in time, was known as Wapping-on-the-Woze (meaning Wapping in the mud) because of its marshy environment. There are two possible theories for the name Waeppa. Either it derived from the Old English word 'wapol', which means marsh, or it is the personal name of a

Saxon chieftain. The first idea is currently the preferred one as there is no other evidence of someone named Waeppa, but this side of the story is possible. Later on in time, Wapping became the little village-like part of London it is today.

Going back to this legendary local, Captain William Kidd (1645 – 23 May 1701), was considered an outlaw. He was the longest living pirate, but was hanged at Execution Dock after being caught. His wife, Sarah Kidd, was his accomplice, and they sailed the seas. The captain's most notable achievements as a pirate was capturing the *Quedagh Merchant* ship. This was where he got his treasure. The ship was an Armenian merchant vessel and where the ship ended up remained a mystery until 2007 when the remains were found.

A mudlarking treasure linked with pirates are 'pirate cob' coins, as these maritime raiders would ransack Spanish ships headed to the Caribbean and steal their treasure chests. They might have ended up in the Thames if they were captured abroad and brought to London for a trial at the High Court of the Admiralty. If found guilty, pirates were paraded across London Bridge before being hanged at Execution Dock, which lay behind what is now the Prospect of Whitby pub. A replica of the noose is still seen standing in the same spot.

Clues to the past

Relics from all time periods can be found scattered along the Thames. Much of written history began with the Romans who laid the foundations for the city today. Then the Vikings who raided what would later become London. Following these warriors, the Elizabethans, Jacobeans, Edwardians, Victorians and Georgians, along with everyone before, between and after. All of their history—and its secrets—are hidden in the banks of the River Thames.

The treasures we find today on the foreshore reveal how people lived and the kind of jobs people held in former times. The time of the original mudlarks was during the industrial revolution and before the First World War. During the Industrial Revolution jobs included working in factories in the bigger cities like London, often under dangerous conditions. Mills were common too. In addition to crafts and small-scale manufacturing, the city was overcrowded and lacked good hygiene. The city was filled with slums, from the west to the east of London. There were outbreaks of diseases such as typhoid, cholera and scarlet fever. Anyone could catch these illnesses, but when many people exist in a small space disease passes easily from person to person. Further afield, mines could collapse at any moment, and in cotton mills little pieces of thread would float around in the air causing people to have difficulty breathing. Sometimes these respiratory issues became fatal. When other machines came into use, limbs and fingers could get stuck. Even in these grim conditions, it was often children (mudlarks back then were usually aged between 8 and 15) and women who had to traipse through the mud, which was sometimes knee-deep, in the hopes of finding something of value to sell so they could make a living. It was one of the only jobs available to the poorest part of society.

In 1850, these mudlarks would typically only make about eight to twelve pence a day, which was not much even back then. They often looked for coal and rope, or copper nails, as all those items were sellable to the general public. These mudlarks searched for the goods with their eyes, hands and feet in the mud, hoping to find something of value. They didn't usually have big tools they could use for digging so they would have to feel around with their toes. There is a good chance they felt a crab bite their foot a couple times! They needed the money to buy necessities like food or clean water and depending whether the river gave some treasures they might not get dinner that day…

It was also very dangerous. They didn't have tide charts available to them and could get cut by glass hiding in the mud, along with other sharp objects they couldn't see. The cleanliness of the water wasn't too good back then either. The Thames was acting like a rubbish dump, which eventually led to the Great Stink of 1858.

During a hot July summer, the stench became unbearable. The sewage included untreated industrial waste from factories and other workplaces, and human waste. Soap and chemicals were ending up in the river, harming the environment. The solution to this problem was a new sewage system, which we still use today – with recent modifications.

Some other professions found along the Thames in the past included watermen, garthmen and lightermen. Then, of course, there were also dockers and warehousemen. Back on the river, there were also dredgers who would be looking for items that had fallen overboard, as there was flotsam and jetsam to be found.

However, nowadays mudlarking isn't usually done under harsh circumstances. Mudlarking is now a fun recreational activity or hobby which many people discovered during the pandemic, though its popularity was already rising again in the 1970s. The '70s and '80s can be called the 'golden age' of mudlarking. This was when the PLA was starting to give permits to mudlarks and allow them onto the foreshore, though with restrictions like filling in any large holes you dug. But, it might be easier to find treasures nowadays as the waves from the Thames Clippers bring up a lot of objects the tide alone might not have brought us. Mudlarking has seen a surge in popularity in the past few years, making the foreshore a busier place. Some Londoners remember going down to the foreshore as a child looking for oyster shells and pieces of slate which are still common finds today. And now, you found it too! If you are new to mudlarking, welcome to the foreshore—which more often than not, opens a portal to the past.

Becoming a time traveller

While modern mudlarks still hope to find a gold ring and silver pendant, other objects like pipe bulbs and pottery are prized possessions from the past. Mudlarking is like a bridge between the old and the new. On the foreshore you can find Roman coins lying next to a broken beer bottle that still has its sticker on it. Mudlarking closes the gaps in the stories we are told. In London, at the foot of historical landmarks like Shakespeare's Globe and Tower Bridge, it almost feels like you can step back in time—be like a time traveller.

London itself started as a Roman civilisation around 2,000 years ago centring around the river. Rivers were always vital for early settlements as they provided water and a food source and transportation. Every major city is likely to have a body of water. Back then it was called 'Londinium', which we also now call Roman London. So the Romans founded the city before it was handed over to the kings and queens, while gradually growing into the diverse city it is today. A city we can explore while mudlarking in the footsteps of the past. Christopher Wren (who designed the modern St Paul's Cathedral) wanted to make the River Fleet navigable again so that more of London and the Thames could be scoured for their pasts. The Fleet river runs for about 6 kilometres from Hampstead into the Thames. It is almost entirely underground with the city on top of it now, but at certain points along its path you can hear, see and smell it travelling underneath your feet through the grates. There are even special soundwalks you could venture on, such as *Fleet Footing*, if you would like to learn more about the history of this hidden river. You used to be able to see it splurge into the Thames by Blackfriars but with the new sewage system, it flows into the sewers instead.

After the Great Fire of London in 1666, much of the city, including St Paul's Cathedral, needed rebuilding. Before the fire, there was Old St Paul's Cathedral—it is unrecognisable when compared to the one standing today! The old cathedral was already in disrepair when the city went ablaze, but after the Great Fire, Christopher Wren was commissioned to design an entirely new building. St Paul's is now famous for its beautiful dome (which made it the tallest building in London from 1710 until 1963) and its choir school. After the fire, the king had decreed that there should be a continuous 'Thames

A bird's eye view of a mudlarking trip's treasures, featuring pieces of pottery, pipe stems and broken bulbs, glass and broken pieces of shell. (*E. Vaxby*)

A view of the River Thames from the foreshore outside Tate Modern, with St Paul's Cathedral. (*E. Vaxby*)

Quay' along the north side of the river. This was meant to replace the messy riverscape. But before the Thames Quay could be built, unplanned quays had been erected so the plan was never put into action as intended.

The word 'mudlark' is a straight compound word of 'mud'—the sediment our ancient artifacts are kept safe in under the River Thames—and 'lark'. During the eighteenth century, it was also used as a slang term for a pig. A *mudlark* is also the name of a magpie-lark. Magpies are birds that search for treasure too. Back in the day, a hyphen was often added to the word 'mudlark', creating 'mud-lark', which we have now joined together.

Activities similar to mudlarking include beachcombing, fossil hunting and metal detecting but I think mudlarking is the best! In my opinion, it is the one where you can learn the most about personal stories from long ago. Metal detecting and magnet fishing often only brings up objects like modern rings (please remember, magnet fishing is not allowed on the tidal River Thames). The tidal Thames reaches for approximately 69 kilometres. I know people who love metal detecting but I prefer searching for treasure without a constant beeping, even though it can get quite meditative. You can only really do beachcombing by a beach and, since I am based in central London, I have to travel quite a bit to get just a couple of hours of searching by the sand, while the Thames is five minutes away. It really depends where you live! But these mudlarking skills can be transferable to any of the other activities I mentioned. They all require a sharp eye and a bit of knowledge prior to your trip. Now that I have given you a first insight into mudlarking, let's begin!

Be a mudlark

Mudlarking is something anyone can enjoy. It takes time to learn the ropes of the ship and what your favourites spots are, but through mudlarking you can learn about your local history and reconnect with it. My all-time favourite spots—and where I started mudlarking—are Wapping and Limehouse on the north side of the River Thames. In Greenwich, which is across the river, there are lots of other lovely finds but the stairs are often too muddy to even get down! West London also hosts many good mudlarking spots. Anything and everything can be found along the banks of the river Thames: buttons, marbles, bowls, bullets, nails, cutlery, porcelain figures and toys, badges, shoes, bones and all kinds of sea glass.

By scraping and searching the surface for these long-lost fragments next to the Thames, we can hunt for history. Mudlarks will look over the same spots over and over, always finding new things. For a while I visited the foreshore every single day and there were always new treasures thrown up by the tides. Though we can't dig much with a standard PLA foreshore permit, we can find treasure, just with our naked eye. Some spots can be better than others though. It all depends on where the currents lie underneath the surface of the Thames.

Did you know that in some parts the River Thames is alternatively called the River Isis? The Celts called it the Tamesa, which the Romans made into Thamesis. The part of the Thames called the Isis runs from its source in the Cotswolds until it meets the Thames in Oxfordshire. The union of these two rivers forms the river's full name, Thame-Isis or the Latin name for the Thames. Now we just call it the River Thames. It has over thirty tributaries and is the longest river in England, starting in the Cotswolds before making its way through London to the North Sea. The source of the river is near Kemble (a village in Gloucestershire) by Thames Head. It then runs through Oxford, Reading, London and many other villages and smaller towns. The Thames plays a role in all of these cities' histories but is especially known in London.

London Bridge, Tower Bridge and Blackfriars Bridge all cross the city's river, each one of them rich with stories. London Bridge, for example, was bought by an American in the twentieth century and dismantled to be shipped across the big pond. What we see now is not the original. Many will know the 'London Bridge is Falling

A picture from Millennium Bridge; a great place to play Pooh Sticks! (*E. Vaxby*)

Down' song, but did you know that there are more verses after the famous one? They talk about what material should be used to build the new London Bridge with. They start by suggesting silver and gold, but they have none. Then they move onto needles and pins, then wood and clay and finally land on stone 'so strong' because it will 'last so long'. All things you could find mudlarking!

Going back even further in time, traitors' heads were lined up along the bridge as a warning to others. However, there was nothing like that on Tower Bridge which was opened more recently in 1894 by the Prince and Princess of Wales, who would later become King Edward VII of England and Queen Alexandra. Blackfriars Bridge also brings discoveries. In 1962, during the construction of Blackfriars Bridge, a Roman barge-like vessel was found! It was most likely used as a cargo ship in the busy Roman port. Similarly, in 1910 a Roman boat was found during the excavation work for County Hall near Westminster Bridge. In total, there are about thirty bridges on the tidal Thames. The oldest one still in use is the Richmond Bridge and is from 1777, while the newest construction is the London Millenium Footbridge from the 2000s.

A game often played on bridges is Pooh Sticks. The name is related to Winnie-the-Pooh, one of A.A. Milne's famous characters. It needs at least two players, each with their own stick. The players stand on a bridge above a river and throw their stick into the moving water at the same time, and the first stick to come out the other side wins! This might not work on most bridges in Central London as they are very wide and high up and have a lot of ongoing traffic, but you could try it out on the pedestrian 'Wibbly Wobbly' Millennium Bridge which links the Tate Modern with St Paul's. Just mind the passing boats and fellow mudlarks underneath. Good luck!

2

Meet the Mudlark

My name is Emmylou Vaxby, but I go by Emmylou the Mudlark online and here is how it all started.

As I mentioned earlier, the first time I went mudlarking was when I was very young, around the age of 5 or 6, and my best friend's mother took us both down to the foreshore in the Wapping and Limehouse area in East London to look for pottery and glass. I remember loving it so much—I still have all of my first finds in a special box safely stored by my more recent finds. In there are pieces of china and frosted glass, plain pottery and quite a lot of broken pipe stems which were part of the tobacco pipes that people use to smoke. As a young person, I think it is so important to learn about the stories connected to these objects, of the people who came before us and on the foreshore is the perfect place to unfold these dense layers of history.

Then, a couple years later in 2020 came the Coronavirus pandemic which no one will ever forget. In the UK, we were only allowed out for an hour a day and, for those short sixty minutes, my family chose to go down to the River Thames! It was a chance for fresh air and felt like a mini-vacation while we were all cooped up in our houses. We didn't really ever see anyone on the foreshore at the time, so it was safe to venture there while the virus was circulating.

An image of the foreshore by Limehouse, taken from above. (*E. Vaxby*)

At first, I didn't know that much about what you could find by the river, so I spent my afternoons researching mudlarking and its history. I started logging everything on my blog in May of that year and have been doing so, on and off, ever since. I remember telling my friends about my cool new website and they were following along with my finds at home. As I learnt more about mudlarking, I found that we needed a licence to continue searching of the foreshore so my parents then got a licence and I got one when I became eligible at 12 years old.

At first, I mainly picked out big pieces of glass and pottery—things that stood out a little from the sand and tiny pebbles lying around. Maybe some cool rocks here and there ended up in my plastic bag too, but as I got better at catching the odd things in the mud, my collection had more and more variety: pipe bulbs emerged, along with bottle stoppers and beautiful pieces of pottery each with unique designs.

I think something else that drew me to mudlarking was how it isn't your usual hobby like knitting or tennis. It is different, and anyone, young or old, can have a go. Mudlarking gives you a little peek into a world before our life began, all on the Thames, which no one knows is there: try asking your friends 'what's mudlarking?' and see how they respond. People usually have no clue what it is or use a bit of logic and relate it to something to do with mud, but that's usually as far as they get. My answer to the question is that

Below left: A Covid-19 test back from lockdown which ended up in the Thames. (*E. Vaxby*)

Below right: A bird's eye view of a small section from the foreshore near Limehouse with many rocks and pebbles. (*E. Vaxby*)

it is the act of scavenging the River Thames for historic objects of value, though they still look back at me slightly confused.

I have, however, been mudlarking ever since 2020 so I have gained over half a decade of experience. At first we went down daily as our permitted 'hour outside', but now I go almost every other weekend when the tides align with busy schedules. Sometimes I also attend mudlarking talks. You would be surprised to find how many there are in the mudlarking community! In 2021 I listened to Nicola White, a fantastic mudlark in London, talk about all her best finds from the Thames at a Totally Thames event. I had only been mudlarking for a year so my passion had grown, but I still had a lot to learn like being able to date pipe bulbs by their shape. I was 9 years old at the time and as mudlarking isn't covered much in the national school curriculum, this talk was very inspirational and informative for me. It was the first time I could learn about mudlarking in person instead of just from a screen.

With all of that being said, the internet has thousands of resources that can help you find what you are looking for to expand your knowledge! But sometimes, the treasures decide to remain a mystery. For example, I have found a pipe bulb with a strange sort of hat engraved into it and I am still trying to figure out the story behind this curious symbol.

The plastic free community

Around the same time, in 2021, I also started Wapping's Plastic Free Community which stemmed from a wish to do something about all the plastic I saw on the foreshore while mudlarking. I was once mudlarking with a friend and we saw an elegant white swan looking for its lunch. Then the swan took a jab at a piece of plastic which was floating on the surface. It would have looked edible, like its usual meal. This was all quite upsetting. After I learnt about Surfers Against Sewage, which is an organisation in the UK fighting for better water quality, and found that there was no Plastic Free Community in my immediate vicinity, I decided to start one.

A swan swimming past Stepney Beach. (*E. Vaxby*)

Surfers Against Sewage was founded in 1990 and started with a group of Cornish surfers who were tired of getting sick from the sewage in the sea. It has now grown into a huge organisation, helping to make a difference in our environment. Whether through raising awareness, hosting events or creating a hub of information, they are helping fix our sewage problem. Since 2022 I have often attended the annual Wapping Summer Shindig with my mudlarking-inspired business which fundraises for the PFC (Plastic Free Community). Greta Thunberg was an inspiration to me because of how much of an impact she was making, even though she was so young. Earlier, in 2018, I went on a march through London which she organised. We started by Parliament and slowly made our way off to Trafalgar Square where my family then broke away from the crowd so I could get back to school. I was only 7 at the time, but it had a big impact.

So, you could say I also have a passion for the environment and it goes well with mudlarking. I like organising clean-ups in my local area or tagging along to one of the WaSh (Wapping and Shadwell) Wombles litter picks. The WaSh Wombles are another small organisation in East London helping to clean up the streets. Danny

A look inside a rubbish bag, full of plastic some others and I collected on the foreshore in Wapping after the swan incident. (*E. Vaxby*)

there will have all the details you need to know so that you can join in the fun! The Lower Regents Coalition also does great work on canals. Their social media can be found online if you would like to learn more!

Near Wapping there is Shadwell Basin where you can watch coots and swans make their nests and Canada geese swim around. This is actually very close to the steps I take to go down to the foreshore so I sometimes take a stroll around the basin after a mudlarking adventure. When not outside in the sunshine enjoying observing ducks or landscapes, I take care of my two Eastern Hermann's tortoises who have been staying with us since September 2023. Their names are Mango and Teal and they were born in Brighton.

Above: Some coots (adult and cootlings) swimming around on the Ornamental Canal in Wapping. (*E. Vaxby*)

Below: Swans swimming on the Thames away from Canary Wharf, past Limehouse. (*E. Vaxby*)

Their dad is 110 years old! Tortoises were already being transported to London as pets hundreds of years ago and there was a big boom after the Second World War, though it's all much more regulated nowadays. When living in the right conditions, the average lifespan is 80 to one 150! Some individuals have been known to live up until 200 years, outliving their owners by decades.

Tortoises are very similar to turtles which were used in a very popular eighteenth- and nineteenth-century dish: turtle soup. The shells of turtles can be found while mudlarking on the River Thames. Turtles are not native to the English river, but non-native terrapins (which are very similar to turtles and tortoises) have been previously spotted.

More Mudlarks

There are many mudlarks hunting for treasure on the Thames, like Nicola White and Lara Maiklem ('the London Mudlark'): two very experienced and talented mudlarks who have fabulous collections. You will have read Nicola White's foreword at the beginning of this book. Nicola White was the first modern mudlark I ever heard about and is an amazing role model. She has been mudlarking since her move to London and has found some amazing objects from the past! Her first mudlarking video came to YouTube about fifteen years ago and she is well worth following.

Mudlark Jason Sandy started back in 2012 after learning about mudlarking through television programmes. He has also found brilliant artifacts while mudlarking alongside his work. His book *MUDLARKS: Treasures from the Thames* is full of detailed stories about finds discovered from many London mudlarks. It is great to see how mudlarks are passing on their knowledge to the younger generations. My schoolfriends don't know much about it, but have been following my Instagram page so they are now intrigued to learn more about the Thames' treasure trove. We walk past the river almost everyday when living in London, but most people don't know what is hiding in the mud.

Hidden entrance to Stepney Beach by Limehouse. (*E. Vaxby*)

Let's have a look at some famous mudlarks from the past. The true originals. The ones for whom mudlarking was the way to survive. Peggy Jones was mudlarking by Blackfriars Bridge in the City of London during the 1800s. From what we know, she was a middle-aged woman who was very poor. Peggy Jones' portrait can be found across the internet. However, there are written descriptions of her looks, which say she had red hair and legs encrusted with mud. She hasn't left many other clues since she was last seen in 1821.

Shadwell is an area in East London near the river, also known for the Shadwell Dock forgeries. Between 1857 and 1870, it is where William 'Billy' Smith and Charles 'Charley' Eaton said they had found numerous valuable items. Charley was a mudlark when he was a young boy. These lads found that they could make replicas of valuable items themselves so they manufactured an estimated 5–10,000 objects and sold many to deceived antiquitarians. This scandal is infamous for selling these fake artefacts to unsuspecting collectors. As more of London's population became aware of the deception these two men were making, it became harder for Billy and Charley to sell their forgeries in the capital. This led them to start travelling around South East England, trying to fool new buyers. In modern times, these

Above left: A mudlarking spot near Blackfriars, a place where Peggy Jones likely mudlarked. (*E. Vaxby*)

Above right: A piece of blue and white coloured pottery, found in Wapping. (*E. Vaxby*)

fakes are actually sought-after and have become a real collectible themselves! Items can sell for hundreds and hundreds of pounds! Others are in museum collections or in private homes.

There have also been other records of early mudlarks, some of which you can find in Henry Mayhew's book *London Labour and the London Poor*.

However, you can make lots of things with your finds from the riverbed with good intentions, unlike Billy and Charley: little glass sculptures for your windowsill, jewellery for your aunt or even trinket dishes for your daughter's desk. But first, you have to find them.

3

Training the Eye

Mudlarking requires practice, just like playing an instrument, knitting, playing a sport, etc. This practice is what I like to call, *training the eye*! At first, everything will look the same. The pebbles, pottery and pipes will visually melt together. The pipe bulbs become rocks, the pottery becomes sea glass and so on. You will need a good game plan here to win the precious prizes!

Training your eye to find the shimmers in the foreshore rocks will let you be able to spot something special in the riverbed. For example, a glittering rock could turn out to be a beautiful piece of sea glass—sea glass is glass that has been sanded down from it being tumbled around in the waves. Through this process, the broken glass will lose the sharp edges and get a beautiful, frosted look. However, this little trick of mine will only work on a sunny day so it is important to find some other techniques you can use when the drizzly London weather comes back and the sun has gone away again.

Make sure to bend down and get close to the ground. This can assist your hunt for treasures and give you a better chance of spotting something exciting. When mudlarking was first done, it was mainly children who would find the valuable items (which were usually the smallest pieces of gold or silver) because they were closer

Above: A comparison between a large pottery shard and three very small fragments. (*E. Vaxby*)

Left: A piece of pottery among rocks and pebbles. (*E. Vaxby*)

to the ground. The same goes for beachcombing and fossil hunting, two other hobbies which have similarities to mudlarking.

Close to the ground, your eyes will scan and spot even the smallest of pottery fragments—and trust me, these can be tiny, smaller than your fingernail! Any bulbous shapes that stick out for you could even be a clay pipe bulb which is a firm favourite in any mudlark's collection.

Other ways to find the treasures around all of the rocks, sand and debris is to scrape over the surface with your hand, boot or trowel, to see what is hiding underneath. But be careful not to dig too far, otherwise you could end up breaking the PLA's rules about how far you can dig, which is 3 inches, or 7.5 centimetres. Mudlarking is not a public right as all the foreshores in the UK have an owner—this is why you need a permit to mudlark. More about that in the Looking at Licences chapter.

The technique of brushing over the top of the foreshore is my favourite since little pieces of pottery and glass appear when I roll the larger rocks away!

Chances are, every time you go mudlarking you will add something special to your collection. Part of being a good mudlark is only picking up the best of your finds. If you have already found twelve pieces of a light blue sea glass, do you really need to pick up one more? Make sure you don't end up with the whole foreshore at home. Some mudlarks, when going through their treasures at the end of the mudlark, even decide to give some of their finds back to the foreshore by placing them back in the mud. You are also legally required to report any objects that are over 300 years old or have significant historical value to the Finds Liaison Officer from London as part of the Portable Antiquities Scheme. Their contact details can be found online.

Another tip you might find helpful is that there are often interesting things lurking at the edge of the foreshore, where the beach meets the city. This is because large rocks can keep the smaller items from falling back down to the river bed and they often collect

Below left: A tin-glazed plate edge, a piece of green glass and a plain porcelain fragment. (*E. Vaxby*)

Below right: A rocky foreshore. (*E. Vaxby*)

The bottom of a flight of stairs leading down to the foreshore. (*E. Vaxby*)

Above left: Where the wall meets the foreshore in Wapping. (*E. Vaxby*)

Above right: A complete bottle found by my friend during a *Mudlark with Me*. (*E. Vaxby*)

there at the top. Other places to check out are the bottoms of stairs and around the structure of old piers, where exciting finds often get stuck.

To practice mudlarking, you could even make it into a friendly competition with others. This way, you can see what others find interesting to pick up, objects which you might not have known to look out for. It is like finding a new perspective. I have had many little competitions with my younger brother and we always seem to find the best treasures during a contest! You can always learn from others' experiences.

Pace is also an important thing to think about when mudlarking. There are two different styles: slow and steady or fast and sharp. You sometimes use a mix of the two. First, you look quickly around to see if you can find anything sparkling in the sunlight showing you that spot has potential. Next you might walk over there and slowly look in between the rocks, maybe scratching the surface to reveal what is lying underneath. If that area didn't give you anything special, you could either look up quickly again and find a new spot, or walk slowly onwards, with your eyes glued to the ground. I have also had mudlarks where I just stay in one spot for the majority of the time, making sure I have found every treasure that area has to offer.

The foreshore in East London on a foggy day. (*E. Vaxby*)

PART II

RAIN OR SHINE

4

What to Wear

During the late 1700s and early 1800s, clothes would usually be fastened together with straight pins instead of buttons or modern zips. These were often coated in a tin alloy to make them shinier. Many of these straight pins can be found on the foreshore, though often a little bent out of shape. Tens, even hundreds, can be found together, sometimes moulded together. Mudlarks have these objects in multitudes at home. These pins are hard to date by eye but some could even be Roman! They usually only go back to the late eighteenth or early nineteenth century, when the rich women wore beautiful dresses like those described in the works of Jane Austen. Layered clothing with petticoats and undergarments and corsets. The men on the other hand wore waistcoats and similar items that we now associate with Regency England. A three-piece coat, breeches, linen shirts and stockings would have made up much of their wardrobe.

However, the poor mudlarks would wear very different clothing. If a mudlark was fortunate enough to have clothes, then they would be ragged. Scruffy, maybe stained and dirty. But, if they were an orphan for example, they would have no one to care for them or to give them any new clothes. They usually didn't even have shoes!

Nowadays, there are lots of different options for modern mudlarks to choose from in terms of fashion. Remember to prepare

An image of my pink rubber boots while I stand on the foreshore. (*E. Vaxby*)

for any kind of weather. Sometimes, a cold breeze floats along the River Thames which might send a chill down your spine. On summery days, the sun shines upon your face while you are looking for treasures. On these occasions you may wish to wear a cap and sunscreen while mudlarking. In winter, scarves, gloves and woolly hats matched with a waterproof jacket are a must when faced with London's rainy days. In autumn and spring, a light windbreaker or puffer jacket can do the job.

Above: The landscape in Canary Wharf, with bright blue skies above. (*E. Vaxby*)

Below: A picture of rainy London: the river below, a light mist in the air and Tower Bridge lighting up in the middle of it all. (*E. Vaxby*)

Throughout all seasons gum boots and waterproof trousers are key to creating a barrier between the splashes, the mud and yourself. Some people also wear gardening knee pads so that they can kneel down on the slippery surface to spot the tiniest of finds without getting themselves too wet or muddy. You should not wear shorts because something might scratch your leg and that item may not be clean. Going back to the topic of gloves, these can also protect your hands from sharp objects and cuts and grazes while keeping them warm and clean. You can use gardening gloves you might have lying around in your shed or some disposable plastic gloves. When I wear gloves, I prefer to use gardening gloves as they are thicker and can be reused. If you do use the single-use gloves and they are recyclable, make sure to put them into the proper bin.

In general the Thames is a very dirty place so adding this barrier will help ensure that you don't contract anything unwanted from the water. Nevertheless, always make sure to wash your hands after an adventure to the beach whether you have been wearing gloves or not, but also bring some hand sanitiser along and avoid eating and touching your eyes/face before properly cleaning your hands.

For shoes, if you don't have any good gumboots yet, some old trainers that you don't care too much about are good too, but make sure to stay out of the water! My preference will always be pink boots because they stand out among the rocks in the foreshore.

I have actually also found some items of clothing while on the foreshore. Shoe soles are the most common (you can even find Tudor shoes in the mud—more on that later) but accessories like watches and buttons and some very wet fabric are common fashion finds. Cobbler's feet which look quite creepy when sticking out of the mud, are uncommon, but many have still been found. They are usually metal in the shape of a foot and cobblers (people who repair shoes) would use them. These models are also sometimes named 'cobbler's lasts'. A 'last' is a model of a human foot used in shoemaking. These cobblers' feet were probably discarded into the Thames, as they can't have taken a walk themselves to the foreshore!

Above: The foreshore near Wapping Wall in East London on quite a foggy day. (*E. Vaxby*)

Below: The sole of a shoe found on the River Thames in good condition, though slightly deformed at the heel. (*E. Vaxby*)

5

What You Need and What You Might Want

A licence is a definite must-have for mudlarking on the River Thames but I'll talk about that later. Before you get started on your adventures, you do need some other equipment too. Things like a trowel, some containers to store your finds and, depending where you are mudlarking, a sieve might also be helpful.

I mostly use my gloved hands because I enjoy mudlarking on slightly sandy foreshore beaches with pebbles so a lot of digging is not always needed. You can move around rocks, but make sure you put them back after you have had a look to minimise the disturbance to the foreshore. When mudlarking in muddier environments, your treasures might not be visible on the surface so you have to use your trowel to find them. A trowel is a triangular metal blade attached to a handle that you might use to lay bricks, do a bit of gardening—or lift treasures from the depths of the mud.

You will also need something to carry your finds home in. I use an old bag which I keep reusing for other adventures but old Tupperware or other containers are good too. If you are using food containers, make sure their purpose is now solely for the transportation of treasure so that you don't contaminate your food. Tupperware can also be used to store your treasures once you have cleaned and dried them. These types of containers often stack quite

Left: A very muddy day in Wapping, with the foreshore covered in a thick layer of mud. (*E. Vaxby*)

Below: A wooden drawer with all of my finds: organised into pipe stems, pipe bulbs and their fragments, plain pottery, blue-and-white pottery, organic finds among miscellaneous treasures. (*E. Vaxby*)

well in drawers or cupboards protecting your finds until you bring them back on display. I recently sorted through many of my finds into pieces of pottery, pipe stems, sea glass in a variety of colours and my favourite finds.

You can make things with your finds like clay pipe necklaces, sea glass rings, marble bracelets. But please make sure you have a Creative Permit from the Port of London Authority. You can also buy accessories online inspired by mudlarking, like stickers and T-shirts.

When pipe bulbs have been in the mud for a long time, not exposed to the sun or air, they turn a dusty navy colour. When you find a tobacco pipe bulb, which is the end of what was the eighteenth century's version of a cigar, it might be half white and half black. Once you have taken it out of the mud and cleaned it up a little, slowly over time the darker side will turn the colour of light porcelain again. However, the mud might also have stained the clay meaning it will stay discoloured.

A close-up of some of my pipe-stems, all varying in colour. Some are lighter than others. (*E. Vaxby*)

As I mentioned in the previous chapter, after you have finished mudlarking, you are going to want to wash your hands, but that might not be available straight away. I recommend carrying some hand sanitiser for after your trip, but make sure to still wash your hands when you get home. This is because we don't know what is in the Thames in terms of sewage and rats which can carry diseases we don't want to contract. You will also need to clean your mudlarking treasures to avoid them becoming further discoloured from the mud. It also means that your finds are safe to touch and inspect without being worried about germs. For precaution, I usually wash my treasures in a separate sink. This isn't needed but it means I can be sure there is no sand from the Thames lurking on my freshly washed cups and bowls. To clean the actual pottery and pipe bulbs along with everything else in your treasure box, use some dish soap and warm water. Please note, you should not soak ceramic as it can be porous and a soak would make it brittle. Gently rub a soft, damp cloth against the surface of your finds but be very careful, as some things can be fragile. If something is too delicate to handle safely, the best way to preserve your item might be to leave it alone in a safe box protected by wool or something similar. For things like rusty padlocks, you should use a gentle acidic solution to remove the crust. Using ultrasonic waves can do a deeper clean of your finds but machines for this can come with a hefty price attached. If you are looking to check if something you found is made of gold, silver or has a real diamond, testers for this can be found online.

Another technique to help you find coins and other metal objects is the use of a metal detector. This little device alerts you if there is something metallic hiding under the rocks which you won't otherwise have noticed. I haven't used a metal-detector on the Thames before but I know many people who have had great luck when using the tool. However, many treasures are not made of metal, such as pottery or sea glass, so they won't come up when you swipe your metal-detector across the beach. This is why I personally stick to mudlarking but if you do have the metal detector already,

Above left: An image of a wooden structure and some rope in the water near the foreshore by Canary Wharf. (*E. Vaxby*)

Above right: A large metal grid found on the foreshore. (*E. Vaxby*)

give it a go! Please remember to stick to the PLA's rules. They will be sent to you with your foreshore licence.

Trash or treasure

Sometimes you might stumble on something and you are not quite sure whether it is worth adding to your collection. So, you can pose the question, 'Is it trash, or treasure?' At first glance, the answer can feel obvious. If the item stirs something personal in you—a memory or a feeling—then it's treasure by default. The emotional resonance of a find often outweighs its material or historical value. A broken button may not impress a historian, but if it reminds you of the ones on your grandfather's old cardigans, it can become a private heirloom from the river.

But if it doesn't, or you are not quite sure what it actually is, the trash or treasure question might be a bit harder to answer. You could start by thinking about if you have seen an object like it before. Pipe stems and rusty nails make up a good chunk of the foreshore among the pebbles and you can't take them all home! Does it seem very common? Have you already got lots at home? If the answer is no, it is worth putting it into your bag and researching the story behind your mystery find when you get home. The research can bring the reward. But if you already have lots of the same item in your collection, you might want to leave it on the foreshore for another mudlark to find.

In the past, clay pipes were seen as trash after they were used and simply thrown away. But now, mudlarks call them their prized

Below left: An image taken from above of a lone pipe stem among pieces of pottery, rocks, bones and an oyster shell. (*E. Vaxby*)

Below right: A selection of finds from a mudlarking adventure, mostly consisting of blue and white coloured pottery along with two shards with red stripes, the bottom of a brown glass bottle and a light brown piece of pottery. (*E. Vaxby*)

possessions and hope to find them while on the foreshore. What is trash and treasure means different things to different people.

A good way of making sure you only take your best finds home is to spread them all out on the floor before you leave the foreshore. That way you can see all of your most special pieces and the ones you realise don't quite win a place in your mudlarking collection.

Lovely locations

You also need to know the best locations for your searches. My favourite beach is probably Limehouse, though I go to the one in Wapping the most. These parts of the foreshore have a lot of rocks and stones and little pebbles which means you find lots of small treasures. The spot behind the Prospect of Whitby, which is a pub near Shadwell Basin, was the first place I went mudlarking in lockdown. It

During low tide, much more of the foreshore near Stepney Beach is accessible, but only for a short period of time. (*E. Vaxby*)

Above: A view of part of the foreshore by Wapping. (*E. Vaxby*)

Left: The DUPLO sheep found in Canary Wharf during a litter pick. (*E. Vaxby*)

is accessed by steps, though the algae can get slippery if it is raining. If you are looking to find the exact space, it is called Wapping Beach. The Limehouse area—though the foreshore here is technically called Stepney Beach on maps—is my lucky spot. It is where I found my first proper pipe bulbs (the whole story is in Chapter 13).

Heading along the Thames, the area by Canary Wharf is not my all-time favourite as there is usually a lot of plastic, but that makes it a good spot for a clean up instead! It is situated in a little alcove near some piers and somehow rubbish always washes up here. However, it is the spot where I found my DUPLO sheep! DUPLO are children's building block toys and there are some character-type ones too. This sheep appeared during one of my family litter picks in Canary Wharf and I decided to take it with me so that I could give it a rinse and a home.

Other locations can get a bit muddier. The Isle of Dogs, one of my favourite spots, was once known as Stebunheath Marsh, but the modern name's origins remain unclear to me. This location is much muddier than other locations because of where this beach is on the river and how the Thames' currents transport sediments. If you go and it is muddy, you will be properly mudlarking! You can get stuck in the mud so be careful where you step, and always mudlark with someone else who could rescue you. The spot on the Isle of Dogs is definitely the muddiest location I have ever gone to, but it might have just been that specific day I visited. It is important to remember that even if it is a little easier to find hidden gems by the rocks on pebble and sand beaches, it is in the mud that you will find perfectly preserved wonders from the Thames. You just have to know what to look for!

Sometimes if I am looking for a new spot, I will go on an online map's street view and drag along the foreshore until I find some steps or another way to get down to the foreshore. There are sometimes ladders you can use but they never look very safe to me so I prefer to stick to stairs and ramps. I used this sort of process to find the beach by Mudlarks Way near the O2 in Greenwich. The name of the road seems quite fitting! I had heard about a beach in that area and put my detective skills to the test to try and find the new spot. It is near a yacht club so it has a long ramp for foreshore access. Even though no pebble beach beats the best ones in Wapping and Limehouse, I still came home with some wonderful finds from Mudlarks Way!

The name Greenwich stems from the Saxon 'Grenewic' (green town). It has a rich naval history, with the National Maritime

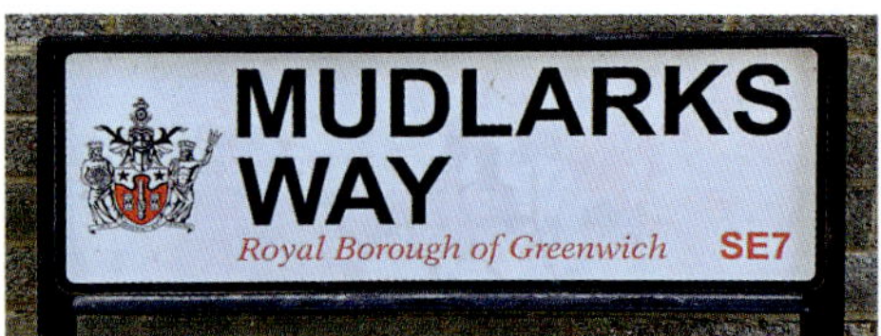

A street sign for Mudlarks Way in Greenwich. (*E. Vaxby*)

Museum living in this part of London. There is also the *Cutty Sark*. This three-masted ship set sail from Scotland on 22 September 1869. The main mast is 153 feet high and there are 11 miles of rigging. The ship cost £16,150 when it was first built, which would have been as much as £2.5 million in today's money. It has visited sixteen different countries in its lifetime, as far away as China for tea! The *Cutty Sark*, whose name comes from one of Robert Burns' poems *Tam O'Shanter*, has travelled the equivalent of two-and-a-half voyages to the moon and back! *Cutty Sark* is an archaic Scottish name for a short nightie. When the ship was sold to a company from Portugal in 1895, the ship's name changed to *Ferreira*, but the crew still called it 'pequina camisola' which is Portuguese for 'short nightie' just like the name *Cutty Sark*. For a year in 1922 the ship

An image taken on the foreshore of the view from a spot in Greenwich. (*E. Vaxby*)

belonged to another Portuguese company and had another new name, but then Captain Dowman of Falmouth bought the ship and gave the boat its original name back: *Cutty Sark*. You can visit it yourself in London as it is part of the Royal Museums Greenwich.

On the other side of the Thames, near the Tate Modern art gallery, there is the lovely sandy Bankside beach. It is technically called the Thames beach. Though I don't find as many things here, it has a picturesque view of London's famous landmarks: squeezed between London Bridge and Blackfriars Bridge is the dome of St Paul's Cathedral ahead and the tall Tate Modern tower behind you. This location in the centre of town is easily accessible, with ramps leading down to the foreshore. Getting to the location is also simple, you can hop on public transport and take a scenic walk down the South Bank before reaching the foreshore.

It is important to note that you are not allowed on various parts of the foreshore nearby where entry is prohibited with a standard permit. For example—with a standard permit, you must not dig or search Queenhithe Dock, the foreshore adjacent to the Royal Palace at Greenwich and the launch ways of the SS *Great Eastern*. The beach in front of the Tower of London is also unavailable, along with the foreshore within the defined exclusion areas at the Palace of Westminster and 85 Albert Embankment. This permit doesn't give permission to mudlark on any foreshore which is not under the ownership of the PLA or the commissioner. For the most accurate and up-to-date details, it is best to refer to the Port of London Authority's website. Please double check before setting out! As a permit holder, you must also not search or dig within 10 metres of all London passenger piers and operational cargo-handling berths, the Thames Flood Barrier in Woolwich Reach, gas pipelines at Blackwall Point and Beverley Brook, HMS *President* (MoD), the lock entrance to St Katherine's Dock, The London Eye, Thames House and the IMO building at Albert Embankment. In addition, you must be mindful of the nature on all parts of the foreshore! Bearing all this in mind, you are good to mudlark.

Above left: A view from the Millennium Footbridge of the Thames and foreshore, with many people on the beach below. (*E. Vaxby*)

Above right: The imprint of my footstep in the wet sand. (*E. Vaxby*)

The Thames is great for mudlarking, not only because of the protective mud and its tides potentially revealing new treasures again and again, but because of London's diverse history. Each area of the city has its own stories to tell—I am only scraping at the surface of it, but do dig deeper. The Thames lets you discover more about the lives of people than you could ever imagine! I started mudlarking quite young, and as I go through school, it has been interesting to see how the History curriculum differs from what I have learnt from the Thames. History is a fantastic subject, but not everything fits into a high school textbook. While mudlarking and researching your finds, you often discover something about the people from the past, whether weird or wonderful. For example, someone like William Manby who I learnt all about through a simple pipe find. There is more about him in Chapter 13 where I tell his forgotten story.

Chiswick, on the edge of London, can also be mudlarked. I once went there for a trip with the Thames Discovery Programme. I learnt many valuable things about the river's ecosystem before going to look for different types of insects in the mud. I also came across a bottle stop while visiting. Bottle stops are used like corks, to seal the opening at the top. They can be made from cork or plastic (along with some other materials like metal, but they aren't as common) but I find the glass ones the prettiest! I believe the bottle stop I found in Chiswick is a screw stopper. It looks like a regular bottle cap design at the top but then has a sort of screw thing underneath. They are quite common on the Thames. Another design similar to this old bottle stopper design is the chisel shaped thumb screw stopper

A fragment of a broken pipe bulb, found on the foreshore by Wapping. (*E. Vaxby*)

which evolved from the older design. This new stopper was easier to grip with your fingers, making opening bottles a simpler task.

With all of that said, you can apply your mudlarking knowledge elsewhere. I mentioned beachcombing and fossil hunting back in chapter one. Both activities are sort of the siblings of mudlarking. I do these myself when I am on the beach in Belgium during the summer, or on the English coast, and I go out to look for special finds. I have found sea pottery and glass but shark and stingray teeth have turned up a couple times as well. Brittle stars are very common too, but very often just the middle remains on the beach.

Above left: An entrance to the foreshore (Stepney Beach). (*E. Vaxby*)

Above right: The foreshore in Wapping on a muddy day. (*E. Vaxby*)

Shark teeth can also be found on the Thames. The beach back in Belgium is sandy and is cleaned everyday in-season so the chance of finding something that I consider treasure (and the cleaners consider rubbish) is quite low. You can however look for sea life; I have seen seals before, along with masses of jellyfish, starfish and crabs, plus sea urchins (but I don't take any of these home!). I have a little seashell collection which I hope to add to when I travel. Here, too, please remember to stick to local laws about what you can take from the seashore as sometimes removing natural materials like pebbles, shells and or sand is strictly forbidden. The reason behind this is often to protect the ecosystem or the landscape of the beach.

Shells

I want to focus on shells for a little longer. 'Shelling' (hunting for shells) is a popular hobby in many parts of the world, but not legal everywhere. Looking for shells can be a relaxing activity once in the summer, or something that you do everyday if you are lucky. Different species of shells live in different parts of the world. In Britain, the common cockle is considered the easiest to find on beaches. This same type of shell is also the most common one in Florida, for example, while limpets are a frequent find in California. When you think of a shell, you will most likely envisage a scallop (the quite flat shells with a scalloped edge) or some sort of whorl shell (the 'twirly' ones). Conch shells (found in the Bahamas, the Caribbean, Florida Keys and Bermuda) and cowries (often used in beach jewellery) also spring to mind. But other shapes exist too, like the rectangular razor shells which can be found in the United Kingdom. I have found quite a few of these in Europe too. But identifying shells can be tough as there are over 100,000 species of molluscs! Shells themselves are made from calcium carbonate. They do 'grow' but not by themselves. The creature living inside will continuously add more layers to the shell, making it larger and larger. This accommodates the molluscs' growing bodies.

A selection of foreshore finds, including part of a coconut, some shells, some pottery, a tooth, a fragment of glass and more, all in a small basket. (*E. Vaxby*)

PART III

DOS, DON'TS AND DETAILS

6

Possible Dangers

While mudlarking uncovers so many beautiful stories from history, it is also dangerous and before stepping onto the foreshore, you need to know all of the dos and don'ts. Otherwise, you could put yourself in unnecessary danger!

First of all, try to always go down to the beach with someone else. If this is not possible, make sure to tell someone you are going down and what time you can be expected back. Update them with your phone which you should always have with you in case of an emergency. If you haven't quite turned 16 yet, going with an adult is a must. The PLA itself says that anyone under the age of 16 must be supervised by an adult while on the foreshore.

Before going on your adventure, look on a map where two entrances to the foreshore are. This means that if the tide comes up too quickly and blocks one, hopefully the other can still be accessed. Tides are very dangerous and you need to be aware of when the water is coming up. This information can be easily accessed on live online tide charts, giving you a forecast of the next few days. Forecasted tides are very helpful when planning out when you want to go to the foreshore, but they can take an unexpected turn too. I will talk more about the science behind them in the next chapter.

Above left: An old telephone with its back missing in front of a toy shaker, a complete green bottle, two golf balls and a piece of a metal grid – all foreshore finds. (*E. Vaxby*)

Above right: A broken wooden staircase missing the steps. An unusable entrance at Wapping. (*E. Vaxby*)

The Thames is also very cold, so if you get swept away, it can be very dangerous. The fast current can take you far out and pull you under, even if you are a strong swimmer. This is why you should never enter the water, which is full of hidden currents and unexpected objects.

Some mudlarks carry a whistle which, if you were ever in great danger, you could blow to alert someone's attention. Since we are in London, one of the busiest cities in the world, there would most likely be someone around who could get help if it was needed but it is better to be safe than sorry!

Apart from the tides, the Thames also brings other dangers. Sharp fragments of glass can cut you, which is why it is also important to wear thick gloves. Thick-soled shoes are also good as nails and medical waste like syringes, even knife blades can protrude through other materials easily. It is also important to never pick things up if you don't know what they are. This is because there are still some grenades around from World War II, though they are quite rare. In a situation where you come across such an object, alert the police and they can handle the situation. You should also tell this service if you find any other weapons like firearms, making sure to follow the law.

Britain entered World War II on 3 September 1939, two days after the invasion of Poland. A year later, there was the Blitz where the Nazis hit major British cities. In London, landmarks like Buckingham Palace, St Pauls and the Tower of London were heavily targeted and bombed, but managed to survive. The Docklands, however, were severely damaged. The end of World War II in Europe was declared on 8 May 1945, known as VE Day.

Below left: An alleyway leading to Wapping's foreshore. (*E. Vaxby*)

Below right: Spot on the foreshore in Wapping where a dead rat was found. (*E. Vaxby*)

Another danger to look out for are the rats, pesky little creatures which inhabit almost every corner of London. They are a frequent sight when walking along streets, usually scurrying away before you get too close. Though pet rats are cute, the same doesn't go for the ones by the foreshore and in the underground sewers. Leptospirosis (Weil's disease) can be contracted from these rodents as they do their business everywhere. The symptoms of this illness are: a high temperature, headaches, body aches and pain, stomach aches, redness/yellow in the white part of your eyes and yellowing skin. There is a chance of catching this disease when on the Thames. It is therefore vital that you disinfect your hands after every trip and if you do show any symptoms, visit your GP. To avoid getting infected, make sure you cover any open wounds too.

Furthermore, the surface can be uneven along the foreshore so you should mind your step! The algae, water and mud can make rocks very slippery. You should always be looking where you are going and not walk backwards. Running on the foreshore also poses some serious issues with health and safety. Tripping on something or getting stuck in the mud can result in a twisted ankle or worse!

Getting down to the foreshore can also be quite nerve wrecking, as the steps might still be wet or covered in green algae. This can add risks. If available, hold onto a banister or the wall and slowly climb down the steps, but only if you think you can do it safely. Bear in mind you will have to come back up them later! Ladders are also a way down to the Thames, but I prefer to stick to the steps as they look a little less dodgy. However, ladders are a very handy way to get down to a specific spot, just make sure they are safe and sturdy.

Why don't we talk about some of the dangers to wildlife too? As humans, we have completely changed Earth's landscape and in some places are continuing to destroy it. We are pumping our waste into the river and this is damaging the environment. So, there are dangers for the environment too by humans meddling with the foreshore. Make sure you leave no rubbish behind. No bottles, no packets, no cans. Only footsteps which already alter the landscape enough.

Above left: The entrance to the foreshore at Wapping. There is a lifebuoy on the open metal gate, leading down to stone steps. (*E. Vaxby*)

Above right: A look inside a bag full of rubbish, filled with trash found on the foreshore while mudlarking. Wrappers, a shoe sole and bottle make up the contents. (*E. Vaxby*)

The river will know you were there! You should leave the foreshore exactly how you found it, except without a couple of its treasures. If you are able to, you might want to pick up any litter you spot. I always carry an extra rubbish bag with me for any pieces of plastic I might see.

7

The Tides

Most of us have had a glimpse of the mighty Thames—whether you have seen it through a window, from a plane or on TV. You might also have hummed along to *London Calling* from The Clash who sing about how we live by the river. But, have you ever wondered why sometimes it looks like it is filled to the brim and other times there are lots of little beaches along its pocket-like banks? It almost looks like someone pulled the plug and the river has been drained. But what is it really?

The Thames' tides are constantly changing and depend on many little things. Generally, there are two high tides and two low tides every day, when the water rises and falls up to 7 metres! That is roughly 23 feet, like a two-storey building! This is what we see visually. The ebb tide describes the tide flowing out to sea (falling to low tide) while the flood tide means that the water is flowing back inland with the water level rising (to high tide). The flood tide deposits new silt on the foreshore and washes objects out of hidden layers. What the ebb reveals, the flood will reconceal. But beware! It cuts off access to and from the foreshore quickly, sometimes leaving people stranded. This process is constantly altering the foreshore. Ebb tides are crucial for mudlarks to do their magic. If there were no tides, there would be little mudlarking magic. We mudlarks

Above: A view from above of the foreshore in between Limehouse and Canary Wharf while the tide is on its way up. (*E. Vaxby*)

Opposite: A circular arrangement of some foreshore finds from Wapping Beach, including pottery, stones and glass (clear and green). (*E. Vaxby*)

need tides so that new things are unearthed for the foreshore to be constantly changing or else it would have been pecked clean from treasures by now.

Tides are the result of the rise and fall of the North Sea. They are caused by the gravitational pull of the sun and moon. When these two giant spheres in space align, we get extreme high tides. These are commonly called spring tides (an informal term is the

A view from the Thames foreshore. A flock of birds are seen flying over the Thames here at Stepney Beach. (*E. Vaxby*)

'king tide') and are experienced after the equinoxes in March and September. Neap tides also cause extremely high and low tides. Did you know that a month is also related to the cycle of the moon?

Storms can bring extreme tides too, sometimes revealing a new untouched section of the beach. When mudlarking during a storm, make sure to always follow guidelines and stay safe. It is also best to mudlark during daytime because it is a lot easier to see what is around you but some people like night-larking when the city has gone to sleep. For that, you will need a head torch and be in the know for what to look out for. You might want some more experience mudlarking first before you try it in the dark.

As you might have guessed, you can only mudlark at low-tide. This gives you about a two-hour window where you can explore the

Thames' beaches. But, what actually is a tide? Tides are the rhythmic rising and falling of sea levels, mostly because of the sun and moon's force as explained.

Sometimes we have a lot of heavy rain in gloomy London. The amount of precipitation has an impact on the level of the water in the river. This will make the river swell simply because there will be more water in the Thames as more of it is on the ground. When standing at the edge of the banks at high tide, you may find there is only a metre or so between you and the river. Maybe even less! The Thames Barrier is a relatively new construction in comparison to some of the other structures (like the bridges) along the Thames. It was officially opened in 1984 by Queen Elizabeth II and helps control the level of the river so that London doesn't get washed away. The river has been manipulated and shaped to fit around human activity as it travels through the land on its way to the sea.

8
Finding Out More

It is important to do research before mudlarking to be aware of dangers and restrictions along with what you might find. As mentioned, this is because some areas of the Thames have restricted access or you are simply not allowed to go there. This can be for historical value reasons or because of ownership. Even with a licence from the Port of London authority, you may not have access to these areas and going there would be trespassing. Another reason you may not be allowed to mudlark there is because the surrounding structure could be unstable.

It is important to always obey all of the rules when on the Thames because they are there to keep you safe and protect the history of the foreshore. The PLA's website has all of the details you need to know.

You should also learn about what things on the foreshore look like so that you can identify them when scanning across the surface. Mudlarking YouTube videos, like my own, can be very helpful as this shows you what the process of finding treasures is like. Books like this one are also important as it gives you a reference that will always be in your hands, even if a video or article is taken down. There are also a lot of mudlarks who are now sharing their stories on social media so if you want to meet the mudlarking community, that is a great place to start. YouTube and Instagram, two platforms

A wooden structure by Wapping. (*E. Vaxby*)

currently very popular, have lots of mudlarks online that you can easily connect with if you so wish.

It is extremely fun to research your finds after mudlarking. Once you find something interesting on the Thames, like a piece of pottery with writing or a pipe bulb with a certain design, you may wish to research the story behind those pieces. It is all good to just go to the foreshore and find beautiful sea glass and have a bit of fun, but learning about the history of those precious fragments brings you more knowledge and you will end up enjoying mudlarking even more. As a young person, it can be hard to learn about the past because we are moving into the future so quickly. But by stepping back and learning about these objects, we can put modern times into perspective and uncover more about the history of everyday life in the area.

To do this, you can start by simply typing a description of your find into a search engine. Sometimes, you will immediately find what you are looking for but that is often not the case. You could then have a look at some books like this one or online articles from other mudlarks. With social media, nowadays you could even just post a picture online and an expert might be able to answer your queries. The mudlarking community is always happy to help! As I mentioned a little while ago in Chapter 2, going to talks can be a great way to learn more about mudlarking if you want to step off the foreshore for a moment but going to museums with a mudlarking exhibition is another great way to see what other people have found! Most museums are very accessible, and anyone can go.

Here are some museums, societies and books which can aid with your research on the backstory of a find:

1. Museum of London—specifically the London Docklands Museum. There are temporary exhibitions such as the Secrets of the Thames.
2. Southwark Cathedral—from what I have seen, this is London's only permanent mudlarking exhibition! Other mudlarking events are also sometimes held here.

Some treasures: pottery (including a piece of creamware with a 'barley' pattern), glass and pipe bowls. (*E. Vaxby*)

3. The Society for Clay Pipe Research—they have many publications on their site which can help date your clay pipe and possibly find the maker and design.
4. The British Button Society—they can help identify your button!
5. *A Mudlarking Year: Finding Treasure in Every Season* by Lara Maiklem and *MUDLARKS: Treasures from the Thames* by Jason Sandy.
6. Nicola White (Tideline Art) and Simon Bourne's (Si-Finds) videos online.
7. Other mudlarking blogs such as those on Tumblr, and more mudlarks on social media. With everyone's combined knowledge, you might be able to solve even some of the hardest mysteries of mudlarking.
8. The Thames Festival Trust: Totally Thames Festival is always really fun to take part in. There are a range of events happening in September.
9. Victoria and Albert Museum—all sorts of things: decorations, household objects etc.
10. The Tower of London and Tower Bridge—gives insight into the history of London.
11. The Cutty Sark Visitors Centre—visit one of the famous ships and discover more of the city's maritime history.
12. National Maritime Museum—opened in 1937 and can still be visited today!
13. The British Museum—this museum was the first to cover all fields of human knowledge.
14. The Thames River Police—based in Wapping, this police station sometimes holds open days to learn about the history of the river police.
15. The Ragged School Museum—this museum was part of one of the largest free 'ragged' schools once upon a time and has now been turned into a museum.

There exists an exclusive Society of Thames Mudlarks too where all the mudlarks receive a special licence from the PLA allowing them to dig much deeper.

All of these places and people have some sort of link to mudlarking or London's history. You can find lots of exhibitions (sometimes pop-up and sometimes permanent) where you can gain vast amounts of knowledge about things you might find on the Thames.

As previously explained, you also need to make sure you have looked at what licence(s) you need to mudlark in London. Without the correct licence, you are not allowed to mudlark on the foreshore and there are consequences. In the next chapter I will go into more detail about the PLA's licensing scheme and how to apply for one.

So, those are all of the things you should dig into if you want to mudlark in London.

A muddy foreshore in East London. (*E. Vaxby*)

The foreshore full of pebbles at Bankside in London. (*E. Vaxby*)

If you are not in London, or want to venture outside, you could take a trip to the United States of America where you might be able to have a treasure hunt along some of the rivers there! Make sure to check what permissions you need there too.

If you want something a little closer to home, looking for lost treasures along a beach when on holiday can also be good fun and lets you learn about the local history. As before, there might be rules for this too. For example, taking sand and rocks is against the law in some places.

Random finds. (*E. Vaxby*)

The beach at Brighton. (*E. Vaxby*)

Beyond London, there is also some foreshore searching happening in Liverpool, Bristol and Newcastle where you can often find industrial and maritime items. In the rest of Europe, Belgium and the Netherlands have rivers where you may be able to mudlark. The Dutch have the *strandjutters*, which is the Dutch word for beachcombers. In the past, *strandjutters* were people who searched the shorelines looking for goods from shipwrecks and lost cargo, while today *strandjutten* has become a recreational past-time. You can also do this in India by the Ganges River. There are mudlarks all over the world!

9

Looking at Licences

This part is very important so don't skip ahead. The process of getting a licence can be a bit time-consuming but all worth it in the end when you get to go mudlarking.

The Port of London Authority (PLA) manages the mudlarking permits for London's section of the River Thames. The Crown Estate also owns a large section of the Thames' foreshore. Without a foreshore permit, you are not permitted to search the Thames for any reason or in any way. You may step onto the foreshore without a permit, but you can't take or look for anything.

The reason this permit program is in place is to preserve the historical value of the river so that important treasures don't just end up in a box somewhere undocumented. Any finds that are of great historical interest or value must be reported to the Portable Antiquities Scheme and depending on the age and material must be reported as Treasure.

When receiving a permit, you must also read all of the health and safety regulations which are similar to the risks I outlined earlier on.

So how do you get a mudlarking permit? At the time of writing, this is the process: First of all you have to be over the age of 12 and have a unique e-mail address. This way you can sign up to the

Above: A piece of pottery, blue and white in colour, found in Wapping. (*E. Vaxby*)

Right: The remains of an old wooden structure lying on the Wapping Beach foreshore. (*E. Vaxby*)

PLA's waiting list and eventually you should be given a ten-day window to accept your permit. The waiting list is currently very long but in the meantime, you can take part in group activities like those the Thames Discovery Program holds which don't require a permit.

This is for the mudlarking permit which allows you to search the foreshore and dig down 7.5cm. There may also be other permits you need depending on what you do with your finds. The PLA occasionally issues Creative Permits which are for creatives who want to use their treasures to make things both to sell and for personal pleasure. The artist Alexandra Abraham (@mythamesview.etc) has one and makes beautiful sculptural pieces from mudlarked objects.

Above: A view of Canary Wharf from Stepney Beach by Limehouse. (*E. Vaxby*)

Below: An image of many foreshore finds from Greenwich, all laid out on the sandy foreshore. (*E. Vaxby*)

PART IV

CABINET OF CURIOSITIES

10

Foreshore Finds

Now you have looked behind the scenes of mudlarking—equipment, licences and the tides—it is time to learn about what you can actually find.

The basic objects you want to look out for are shards of pottery, fragments of glass, the bulbs and stems of clay pipe bulbs and common precious metals.

Left: A pink rose which can't have been there very long. An unusual find. (*E. Vaxby*)

Opposite: A collection of treasures found on the foreshore, including a broken telephone, a piece of a coconut shell, pottery shards, glass fragments, a tooth and some pipe stems and bulbs. (*E. Vaxby*)

Now once you know what these look like, they can be recognised quite easily on the foreshore's landscape, but there are other objects that are a little harder to spot.

Any numismatists among you?

Coins from across the centuries can be found on the banks of the River Thames. Modern and ancient. Roman coins are some of the oldest pieces of currency around. The Romans used many different types of coins in their currency, denarii being the most famous.

Other Roman coins are dupondii and gold aurei. The reason we can find coins from the Roman Empire is because the Romans invaded Britain in ad 43. Before they arrived here, the Celts inhabited Britain. It is fascinating how we can uncover so much of Britain's backstory by simply researching coins we found from the Thames! Following the Romans' departure, the Anglo-Saxon Era began with the migration of Germanic peoples from Europe; their Anglo-Saxon language is often referred to as Old English, and is where our modern language, taught all over the world, comes from. They also had their own currency—with gold 'scillingas', silver 'sceat' and later silver pennies—coins which can be spotted on the Thames too.

An item very similar to coins in shape and size is buttons. Buttons began to be used in England in the 1400s but had been used in other parts of the world long before that. Some buttons found on the Thames are simple and plain—they don't have a real story behind them. However, you might sometimes turn over a button, and be greeted by a beautifully decorated piece of metal! You can find sailor's buttons which often have an anchor and rope wrapped around it embossed on the surface. It is understandable that buttons from sailors would be in the Thames as ships would be sailing in and out of London on the river, along with cargo being moved by the docks which are all jobs sailors would have helped with. But buttons from other people in history can also be found as they are an easy thing to lose. Uniform buttons can be found on the foreshore, along with the most common type found by mudlarks: suspender buttons. In general, unless they were very decorative, buttons would have between two and five sewing holes or just a simple loop on the back so that the front could be ornamental. You will have probably already seen buttons like these in your daily life as they aren't very different to modern buttons, just older!

There is another piece of metal I would like to talk about which can often be mistaken for a coin at first glance but is actually a trade token. A trade token, also known as traders' tokens, was primarily used in the seventeenth century due to a shortage of

Above: An image taken while on the foreshore in Greenwich of the pebbly beach and my gumboots. (*E. Vaxby*)

Below: A breaking wave. (*E. Vaxby*)

small-denomination coins, such as halfpennies. Traders decided to create this substitute for official coins. Traders' tokens were usually quite small and made of copper or brass. However, in 1672, it became prohibited to further issue these private tokens so they slowly disappeared from people's pockets.

Thimbles are still used today in sewing. They prevent a sewists fingers from being pricked by a needle. They are often metal and come in a range of sizes, but painted ceramic ones can be found too. The modern thimble comes from a Dutch metalworker working in England in 1695. My mother was the first one to start collecting thimbles in my family. She collected nine in total, each from different parts of Europe. I carried on the collection and now have over twenty thimbles from all over the world. Old thimbles can also be found on the river Thames. Metal ones are the most common as they are the least expensive. There is a thimble in my mudlarking collection, but it came in a rather rough shape.

Something different to traders' tokens, thimbles and coins are inkwells. In the late 1800s and early 1900s, inkwells made of stoneware, called 'porkpie' or 'penny' inkwells, were mass-produced. They were inexpensive and the material they were made of protected the ink from light and moisture. Nowadays we don't really use inkwells in our day-to-day life since gel pens, ballpoint pens and the rest of the items found in a modern schoolchild's pencil case have become so popular. Just as there are different types of pens, there are other types of inkwells you should look out for, like Victorian aqua inkwells made from glass. These Victorian inkwells were made with aqua-coloured glass. It is a clear blue with a bit of green mixed into it. They come in a variety of different shapes but always resembling a cube at the bottom with a neck on top.

Jars are similar to inkwells, but used for a larger variety of purposes. You can find jars for everything: minced meat, pies, pudding—maybe one was used for baked beans! Some types of jars are recognisable and their source can be found from a simple book search, as there are many publications specifically on this subject. Jars can be metal, glass or made from clay.

Lots of glass arranged in the shape of a jug. (*E. Vaxby*)

Now imagine a Victorian lady or gent. Let's say they were writing a letter to their uncle in the north of England. They have finished and just been told their dinner is ready. That dinner may have been cooked in a Victorian pipkin, another common item washed by the river.

Pipkins are small and made of earthenware clay. They usually had a handle and three feet at their base. They look a little like a pan we might use today in cooking but with a more bulbous shape for where you put the food. The pipkins were used to heat food over an open fire or hot coals. It is unlikely you would find a whole pipkin because they are made of ceramics, meaning they are fragile, but you might find pieces of it or even large fragments buried into the mud.

Let's go back in time to an era before the Victorians: Tudor England. Lice were a common nuisance back then, and lice combs from this era, sometimes with nits attached, can be found along the Thames. They are usually wooden with a double comb on either side. The Tudors' hygiene routine was a little different from ours. For example, they did not have toothbrushes so used things like wool to clean their teeth. Shoes, or at least the soles from them, from that time are also walking the foreshore. Through online research you can figure out if it is just a modern shoe you are holding or a very old one. Clues can lie in the shape of the shoe: broad, square shoes with flat soles were the style. The reason why the Thames' mud is so good at preserving things like this is because of its little to no levels of oxygen. The fancy word for this is anaerobic. This level of oxygen makes it perfect for preserving natural things like wood or bone, which I will talk more about soon.

Next topic: shoe buckles (along with belt buckles). If you go into a shoe shop, you will see trainers, formal shoes, maybe some hiking boots too. But there will also be some buckled shoes. Buckles offer a way to close your shoe and secure it tightly onto your foot. Did you know we have been using buckled shoes since around the mid-seventeenth century? Even earlier buckles from belts can be found lying in the mud as well.

Razors are also common, though not that many from today's times. Of course you will find some disposable ones, but add those to your rubbish bag rather than your treasure bag. Razors from the twentieth century are much more well made and can have words on them too. They are usually metal, not plastic.

If you are looking to find something shinier on the foreshore, precious metals like silver or gold can also be found on the River Thames, usually in the form of jewellery. Engagement rings, necklaces, wedding bands and bracelets can all call the riverbed their home. Rings can have a range of decorations, from jewels to engravings. You could even find out about the owner depending what you find on the ring. How did the ring get there? Maybe someone is still desperately searching for it. Or maybe someone decided to throw it into the Thames, to be lost forever. Rings with seals can also be found. These could have been used to easily seal envelopes. These can also be called signet rings and were already mentioned in the Bible! They were also very popular during the Renaissance and Victorian time periods. Fob seals are similar to signet rings. They let the owner easily carry around a personal seal stamp. They are adorned onto something like a watch, pocket or belt. Finally, Georgian brass cufflinks are in many mudlarks' collections too, though usually not in a pair!

Items with a less pretty past like unexploded grenades or firearms can be seen when mudlarking. If you spot something like this, you must report it to the authorities so that it can be handled safely. It is important that you never touch something that you don't know what it is, or that you think could be dangerous. Things like this have been found on the Thames as a lot of bombs were dropped on London (especially in the East End) during World War II, and the river holds all of history's secrets. As mentioned before, the docks and places like Wapping and Bermondsey suffered devastating damage.

But not only the river holds secrets, sometimes you might find one in a bottle too! There are new messages in bottles that use plastic bottles, or old fashioned ones which stick to the famous glass bottle and cork. Inside you can find a simple letter with someone's name and maybe 'have a good day'. There could also be a story: something special that happened to them recently. That little bottle could even hold someone's hopes and dreams. There have even been messages in bottles found with loved one's ashes inside, letting them explore the world by sea.

Something that has become very popular in recent years is geocaching. It is an outdoor activity you can do for fun, where participants use a GPS or mobile phone to find small containers

Left: A look in between some rocks. (*E. Vaxby*)

Below: The foreshore in Wapping. (*E. Vaxby*)

(geocaches) and leave them behind at locations marked by specific coordinates around the world. I have not tried this myself, but I know people who have done a whole treasure hunt looking for these tiny treasures, hidden in day-to-day life.

Back to the messages in a bottle, occasionally the writers of the messages can be traced but they are usually anonymous. This allows privacy for the writer, giving a sense of mystery to the letter. If you find something like this, or something that might resemble a religious offering, it is best to leave it on the Thames as it is not yours to take. On the topic of offerings, the river is shared and might be sacred for some people so sometimes you can spot an offering on the foreshore. Leave it be in peace and carry on with your mudlark.

Padlocks are an unusual find on the Thames, but still quite common. They are often rusty and quite battered from their travels down the river. You never know the story behind them: they could be a love padlock, symbolising a couple's eternal love. There are some areas in London full of padlocks like these. Or maybe, just maybe, the padlock that you have found is from a treasure chest! It is fun to imagine where items like these could have come from, though we might never know for certain.

Padlocks can also be from construction sites. Pieces of scaffolding and pipes are quite common to see on the beach but often too big to move, or take with you! Plus, these objects might not be the treasures you are looking for when mudlarking. Large items can also become tripping hazards so make sure to always look where you are going!

There are often tyres from the sides of barges lying on the foreshore, encased in mud and quite deflated. The tyres probably fell off the boat at some point. They are often used on the sides of boats to protect them as they are cheap and act like a bumper.

If you have ever looked down onto the Thames foreshore, you will have seen a lot of bones. Horse jaws, sheep legs, cow bones and all the rest. One might even find a skull! Human skulls are not common, but still hide among the rest of the bones, ready to

Left: Some bricks on the foreshore. (*E. Vaxby*)

Below: A picture of a tyre on the foreshore. (*E. Vaxby*)

make you jump out of your skin! This is where the river might start sending shivers down your spine as at some points in history, it was not the place you wanted to be stuck in the mud. Due to the strong currents of the Thames, the water has taken many human lives and sometimes even human remains are scattered along the beach. You will only really ever see bones though as soft tissues rot away leaving the skeleton to fall apart, but some grim dead rats have crossed my path before. I have also seen more detached crab legs than I would have liked to!

You might be thinking that if there are so many bones, there might also be fossils? You can find some crinoid stems which look like little coral stars on the Thames, along with ammonites, but they have probably travelled down the river. Ammonites went extinct many millions of years ago, but are closely related to today's squids and cuttlefish. However, there are living crinoids today. A fossil is

A piece of a jawbone, still with some teeth attached. (*E. Vaxby*)

created when a living thing dies and is quickly buried by sediment. The soft tissues decompose leaving behind the hard things like bones and shells. Minerals from water replace the remains forming fossils. Eventually, erosion in the surrounding area will expose the fossil. If you want to go fossil hunting, I recommend visiting the Jurassic Coast in Dorset, or the famous White Cliffs of Dover. I have been to Folkestone a couple times and have many fossils including tiny crinoid stems and some big belemnites (which were also squid-like animals). If you have hunted fossils before, I am sure you will like mudlarking. It puts you in the same headspace letting you search the foreshore at your own pace—as long as you stay aware of the tides.

Opposite: An arrangement of bones on a rock found on the foreshore. (*E. Vaxby*)

Below: A belemnite, a fragment of a crinoid stem, part of an ammonite and an imprint of one. (*E. Vaxby*)

Going back to bones, most of them were probably dumped into the Thames by butchers or chop houses that are now long gone. Other things, like antlers, are a little strange. I haven't spotted many animals apart from swans, geese and cormorants before, but I did once find a little seahorse. It was probably only the length of my pinky and looked alive. There was also a fish in a cormorant's mouth. Mallards and Rouen and tufted ducks are all common waterfowl too. Otters, dolphins and porpoises can also turn up in central London, but are more common downstream in the estuary. But there is a legend, that Richard I returned from a crusade with a crocodile which then escaped from the Tower into the Thames!

While lots of your foreshore finds will be pottery and glass, there are many natural discoveries you can make too. I have found many

Left: A small seahorse stranded on the beach at low tide. Seen while mudlarking at Stepney Beach. (*E. Vaxby*)

Below: A part of a coconut shell. (*E. Vaxby*)

pieces of coconuts in my time, most of which are bigger than my hand! There aren't many coconut trees in London as they are not a native species. So, they are most likely religious offerings, or at least part of one. Coconuts can be a symbol of luck and I think they are often offered to the river as a blessing after a Hindu ceremony.

People from all over the world have immigrated to London. Post-war, there were a large number of people migrating from the West Indies, and these immigrants have become known as the 'Windrush generation' after the *Empire Windrush*, the ship many of them travelled on. If you look at communities in the East End, many residents are from Bangladesh. In the twentieth century, many Bangladeshi men settled in Tower Hamlets to make money to send back home to their families. When their wives and children joined them in London, a whole community was formed. In this area, there had previously been many synagogues because of the Jewish refugees who arrived in the late eighteenth and early nineteenth century. However, now you will find more mosques as many Jewish people moved to the northern parts of the city. The curry houses in Brick Lane owe their history to this community. Spice tins can often be found along the foreshore, along with other types of food packaging.

Further back in the past, around the sixteenth century, many Flemish weavers immigrated to London leaving behind pottery and cloth seals in the Thames. They mostly settled in Spitalfields and around the East End, with the weavers working in small workshops powered by water from streams like the Walbrook and the Fleet. The seals I mentioned, that look like coins, were attached to clothing and other goods for identification and to ensure quality. These lead items began being used in the thirteenth century and then their popularity declined in the nineteenth century. After the Flemish, the Huguenots moved into London in the seventeenth and eighteenth centuries. Their settlement transformed the East End into a hub of fine silk weaving, building on the skills introduced by the Flemish earlier. Silk loom weights and pins sometimes turn up on the foreshore. One hundred years later, during the nineteenth century,

Above: An oyster shell found on the beach in Belgium. (*E. Vaxby*)

Left: A piece of pottery leaning on a shell fragment. Found at Wapping. (*E. Vaxby*)

large groups of Irish men and women also arrived in London due to the Great Famine. They often found their first cheap lodgings at Wapping, Shadwell or Bermondsey. Churches like St Patrick's in Wapping and St Mary and St Michael in Stepney served as a centre of worship and community for the Irish as they were not always welcomed warmly.

Back to some finds, shells are also common, but a lot smaller than coconuts. Oysters add an iridescent shine to the foreshore; they can be found complete or in lots of little pieces. There are living oysters in some parts of the Thames, however, these shells could also have been thrown into the waters from a nearby restaurant. Oysters have been a large part of many diets over the years: these molluscs were very popular with the Romans and a staple dish in the nineteenth century. These shells probably aren't from Emperor Claudius' time! Oysters have two sides to them: one shiny and one slightly duller. The inside will sparkle on the foreshore while the outer surface will hide away. Make sure you are looking for both!

Another type of common shell I frequently see are cockle shells. This bivalve has a round edge and simple design. The ones from the Thames are always plain so I leave them where they are. Whelk shells, on the other hand, are much more fun to find! They are still very common, but much more fragile than oyster and cockle shells in my opinion. They often come with holes! I have found quite a few, with the best spots being in Rotherhithe (Rotherhithe Beach) and Limehouse (Stepney Beach). These areas often have lots of natural waste (shells, rotting fruits). I am not sure how I have seen so many bananas, oranges and apples on the foreshore! Some will just have rolled away from market stalls or been dropped during a riverside picnic. Others may have been part of offerings but are now a meal for the rats!

There are two main types of rat in London: the brown rat and the black rat. They are both non-native UK species as they arrived by ship hundreds of years ago. The brown rat, which is very common, is sometimes also known as the sewer rat. I have heard they are very good swimmers! The black rat is much less common than the brown one. These 'ship rats' as they are also called are a little smaller, but still larger than a mouse. Both of them are considered a nuisance.

I have found a lot of bricks while mudlarking but never taken any home as they are a bit heavy. One brick where I had fun with the research is an LBC brick. LBC stands for the London Brick Company. It is red in colour and is a Fletton brick, now known as the London brick. It was made using Oxford clay and then travelled by train to London where it will have been used for some building, most likely post-war. The LBC faced financial struggles early on, but managed to survive and are still manufacturing bricks today. You can see the word 'phorpres' at the bottom of the brick. This is the brick style—four-pressed. To shape the brick, it was pressed twice in both directions. If you say four-pressed quickly, it becomes, 'phorpres'!

A view from Stepney Beach. (*E. Vaxby*)

I also found a brick in Limehouse with 'WEALDEN' pressed into it, but didn't uncover much history.

And finally, I have a yellow brick which has two lines of text. After looking up 'CLIFF & SON', I found a brick manufacturer. They were called Cliff & Sons and based in Wortley, Leeds, which matches the broken text on the bottom. They were founded by John Cliff around 1795 but Joseph Cliff quickly took over after his father died. He expanded the brick company making him very wealthy. They manufactured enamelled bricks, but Joseph also owned other manufacturers. He started making other things too, such as drain pipes, but brickmaking was his main source of income. Apparently he had fourteen children who married other high-status people, often close relations. He opened a colliery as well. But a while after his death in 1879, there was an explosive disaster killing sixty-three victims. After that, the family continued with other business interests.

Above left: A London Brick Company Phorpres red brick. (*E. Vaxby*)

Above middle: A Wealden brick found near Canary Wharf. (*E. Vaxby*)

Above right: A Cliff and Sons brick found in Wapping. (*E. Vaxby*)

11

Picking Up Pottery

Let's zoom into my favourite topic: pottery from the river. These beautiful splinters of what was once a large ceramic vessel often have smooth, rounded edges with designs I have never seen before painted onto the clay with blue glaze. I think the most common treasure I take home from the Thames is ceramic, as I can never bear to leave any behind! These treasures come in all shapes and forms, some quite big—the size of my hand. I've spotted a whole plate before, though it looked like it hadn't spent so much time in the Thames yet. Other pieces can be smaller than my fingernail and are a trouble to pick up. Ceramics also have different textures—from smooth porcelain and crazed overglazes to rough porous plant pots. Crazed glaze means that there are very fine cracks on the surface of the ceramic piece and can come from many different causes. You can spot it easily.

And so, pottery is a big part of what you find on the foreshore. It is literally part of it! If you go to Wapping Beach on the north bank of the river, you will find a piece of pottery stuck in a rock. You can't get it out! If you used a hammer you might be able to dislodge it, but that would be changing the structure of the foreshore and mudlarks don't do that.

In general, you have lots of different types of clay and glaze mixed together from all over the world; some from here at home in

Lots of blue and white coloured pottery, all arranged on a bamboo mat. (*E. Vaxby*)

Above: A pottery sherd with crazed glaze. (*E. Vaxby*)

Left: A piece of pottery permanently stuck in a rock on the foreshore at Wapping. (*E. Vaxby*)

England but also imports from France for example. English potters often used to imitate the Dutch designs that we know so well.

Pottery can even take us back in time to the Romans! Pieces from an amphora have been found on the foreshore. Who knows, maybe you will find the next piece! The making of ceramics has been around for thousands and thousands of years. Though much of the evidence from these past time periods has gone, traces can still be found.

Some pottery is also a little less interesting, with plain and simple shapes. But this just makes the ones with engravings and colour even more special.

Before we have a look at some of my favourite ceramic finds from the Thames, lets dig deeper into the world of clay. Clay is the substance that makes up ceramic artwork. Creating figurines and other items from this material has been something humans have done for thousands of years; some of the oldest things found on the Thames are over 5,000 years old! This was a skull from the Neolithic period, which came just before the Bronze Age. It was found on the south bank of the Thames by Martin Bushell a couple of years ago. Though it is important to remember that if you find something so old, you must report it to the Finds Liaison Officer at the Museum of London so that it can be documented correctly for the Portable Antiquities Scheme.

Going back to the pottery, clay is ultimately the most important part of it. But there are so many different types of clay and glazes to decorate it with—even different ways to fire pottery!

So let's start near the beginning with Roman Samian ware. This type of pottery was made in what is now France, after production was shifted from northern Italy. Samian ware can also be referred to as *terra sigillata*, though this is a more general term. Samian ware is famous for its smooth surface and is a clay slip that is ultrarefined. Potters still use it today because of its light sheen. This type of pottery can be recognised on the Thames because of its orangey-red colour. The decorations found on sherds of this type of pottery were usually moulded and then applied to the vessel. Samian ware in the Roman times was usually used as fine tableware. It is often associated with high-status but was mass-produced and spread across the Roman empire. Because of its abundance, it was affordable for most Romans. Samian ware is common on the Thames, but you will probably not find it every time you venture down to the foreshore. But when you do, its red gloss makes it very recognisable.

There is also other Roman pottery that can be found on the Thames. Large pieces of amphorae (plural of an amphora—the large wheel-thrown vessel made from terracotta clay) have been discovered on the foreshore. These objects were used for transporting and storing goods, such as wine for example. They

G L O B E W H A R F
Uber

Above: A part of my pottery collection. (*E. Vaxby*)

Opposite: Stepney Beach. (*E. Vaxby*)

were also mass-produced like the Samian ware and were used in everyday life. They had two handles and came in a variety of shapes. Roman amphorae had a range of finishing techniques but were often unglazed. So, if you see a piece of unglazed terracotta pottery on the foreshore, it could be a piece of a Roman amphora! Though, there is a chance it is just a broken modern plant pot too…

The last type of Roman pottery I wanted to quickly mention, is black-burnished ware. As the name suggests, it is black in colour making it quite recognisable on the foreshore. Mudlarks have found lots of fragments over the years making it quite a frequent find.

Moving onto my all time favourite—Delftware pottery. These ceramic pieces are certainly not from Roman times. Delftware is from a city called Delft in the Netherlands. It is famous for its blue and white colour palette, created using the tin glaze technique and often cobalt oxide. Tin-glazed pottery is earthenware which is coated in an opaque white and often decorated in a vibrant blue or other metallic glaze. Inspired by blue and white Chinese porcelain, Delftware originated around the seventeenth century; it was very popular and is still imitated today. The English copied the Dutch and created 'English Delftware', and many potteries along the bank of the river employed Dutch potters. This led to Delftware and china coming to closely resemble each other. Delftware is still made today but can come with a big price tag.

A type of pattern I have found on many of my pieces of pottery from the Thames is fragments of the Willow Pattern. Chinoiserie is a decorative style that uses Chinese motifs. The Willow Pattern, or the Blue Willows, is from England and I believe began to be manufactured in the late eighteenth century. The design usually includes pagodas, willow trees and a fence, along with boats and other elements. It became a very popular design, with many different variations emerging. To help market the design, there was even a romantic backstory created of two lovers who wanted to run away together. It may be based on a true tale, but it was likely created just to add a narrative to the pattern. This design belongs to the transferware category which is a decorating technique. There were many other patterns like this that included other colours too: red, brown and even yellow! However, the most common colour was blue on white.

The next category is Bellarmine bottles. Though I haven't been lucky enough to find one of these yet, these jugs were manufactured throughout Europe and are famous for the bearded man on the neck of the vessel. They are also sometimes called Bartmann jugs, meaning bearded man in German. These jugs have a brownish colour to them and are salt-glazed and are originally from around the sixteenth and seventeenth centuries! They are made from stoneware, which is non-porous (meaning no little holes). Most people only find fragments, but whole jugs have been discovered in the mud. During the witch trials, they were sometimes used to help protect the owners from witchcraft. All sorts of things were

Above: Seven pieces of pottery including a couple of Willow Pattern fragments. (*E. Vaxby*)

Right: Large muddy rocks on the foreshore by Bankside. (*E. Vaxby*)

put inside of the jug which was then sealed with a cork, and these objects can be found still inside when found on the Thames. This is very rare but still possible.

This is one of those things that is on my bucket list to find while mudlarking. I've got the pipe bulbs and other wonderful finds, but this box still needs ticking. Finding things on the Thames needs knowledge and practice so that you know where and what to look for, but also just a bit of luck and hope. Sometimes you will hit a jackpot and come home with something like a Bartmann jug, and other days only a couple pieces of modern glass and a nice rock will come home with you.

Another type of stoneware pottery from Germany is Westerwald stoneware. It is also salt-glazed like the Bartmann jugs but has blue and grey colours instead of brown. I have found a few sherds of this beautiful pottery myself and they are among the most special finds in my pottery collection. They often have raised decoration, meaning you can feel the texture as you slide your thumb across the surface of the fragment. Westerwald stoneware is usually decorated with a striking cobalt blue which contrasts greatly against the grey background.

Some things that can be a little creepier than a plate are china dolls and other porcelain figurines. For example, Frozen Charlottes. These pottery figurines were very popular as children's toys during the Victorian Era (1837–1901, during Queen Victoria's reign). They were dolls created in one piece without joints. They were very affordable, even children with pocket money were able to purchase the dolls themselves. The manufacturing was originally also in Germany, however the dolls were very popular in both England and America, where the Frozen Charlotte name comes from. The dolls are named after an American ballad about a girl who sadly froze to death since she had refused to wear something warmer for a sleigh ride because she didn't want to cover her pretty dress. The ballad is supposed to be about a real girl named Charlotte who, in 1840, rode with her suitor Charlie to a ball. Charlotte arrived, frozen to death and later Charlie died of a broken heart—or so the story goes. Young children played with Frozen Charlotte in all sorts of ways: you could find half-glazed dolls that could float in the bath or some small dolls were sometimes baked into cakes. The doll is a naked girl, usually with blonde hair, rosy cheeks and red lips painted onto her head. The male versions are called 'Frozen Charlies', named after Charlotte's suitor from the story. Many Frozen Charlottes (and Charlies) have been found on the Thames with some mudlarks having whole collections of them!

Creamware also has a pale colour, sometimes even a yellowish glaze, and is from the 1700s. The feather-edge was a popular design for creamware. It looks like little stylised feathers in varying sizes around the rim of a ceramic vessel. Creamware has some of my favourite designs. Creamware often used moulded decorations. One of the moulded plate designs that I have found quite a few fragments of is the barley design. This design centres around the shape of a barley stalk and is often placed in a thick rim around the middle of the plate. The design looks very similar to the Dot, Diaper and Basket design. This pattern—also found around the rim of a plate or dish—was made on a white salt-glazed stoneware, not on creamware, but it used the basket pattern which was very popular for creamware vessels later on. It has 'diaper' in its name because that is what you called a diamond pattern! It also links hand in hand with Pearlware which had more of a blueish tint due to the cobalt that was added to the glaze. Pearlware was what creamware evolved into because people wanted a whiter body instead of the one with the yellowish tint. Pearlware emerged in the late eighteenth century. I have found a lot of pearlware—often 'shell edged'. This design is very distinguishable when displayed against other pottery; first of all because of its very white base and secondly, due to the scallop-like rim. The potter would then usually apply a blue to the rim for decoration.

Most of what I have been talking about were claywares from around the Georgian Era which was from 1714 to 1837. Now spinning our clock backwards and heading to the late medieval period once more, Tudor Green pottery is quite an uncommon find. These ceramics are characterised by the green glaze, which at the time was one of three choices: green, yellow or brown. To be honest, the 'green' glaze is a lot more yellowy than one might think. It is important to note that not all green glazed pottery is from this time period as it was a very popular colour up until a couple centuries ago. Tudor Green is a type of medieval Surrey whiteware. It is named Surrey whiteware because the clay is white-firing and was usually made in the Surrey area, which is south-west of London. Another type of Surrey whiteware is Cheam ware, which had more sporadic (uneven) glazing.

Above left: A barley pattern fragment next to a crazed glaze shard. (*E. Vaxby*)

Above right: Lots of green pottery and glass. (*E. Vaxby*)

You may have noticed that I have called fragments of pottery both shards and sherds. These words can both be used interchangeably but 'sherd' is specifically for broken pottery, while a 'shard' could also be describing glass or other brittle materials. Or even The Shard building in London!

Finally, there is a lot of different slipware to be found on the Thames. I have already talked about the Roman Samian ware, but there is also Metropolitan slipware which is very common. The pottery is usually orangey-red, or even brown decorated with a yellow slip. The decorations are often quite random with squiggles and lines or shapes, but sometimes you can make out some sort of pattern. It is from around the seventeenth century. Though this type of pottery is quite old, you can still find large fragments intact on the foreshore.

Another form of slipware is Staffordshire combed slipware. It is recognisable due to its white to yellow colour with dark slip, which is then combed through while still wet. It is then covered in a clear lead glaze which can be the cause of the yellow tint. It can also be found marbled and/or with a 'coggled' or 'crimped' edge, which I have heard was used to make a uniform pie edge. Staffordshire slipware was originally produced in Staffordshire, which is near Birmingham in the Midlands. This slipware is also from around the mid-seventeenth century to the mid-nineteenth century.

This next topic is a little vague as there are not really any specific designs. I am talking about logos and backstamps and makers' marks. Mudlarking often includes a lot of detective work after a trip to the foreshore and sometimes makers' marks make everything

A collection of pottery finds with various designs, possibly featuring a piece of Westerwald stoneware (bottom left) and possibly some Staffordshire slipware (top right). (*E. Vaxby*)

easier. I recently found a sherd of pottery—it looked quite modern—which had a logo on the back. Unfortunately, it had almost all cracked off except the word 'pottery'. This shows how sometimes the river likes to keep its secrets hidden away, only displaying the obvious truth!

Back to backstamps—these became quite popular in the 1800s. They often included a maker's mark and maybe a location. Sometimes you are even blessed to see a date on there!

Now, spongeware. Spongeware was very popular by the end of the nineteenth century in England, though it is said it was originally from around Glasgow or Edinburgh in Scotland. Spongeware is a decorative technique where you use fine-pored sponge stamps to apply simple pattern designs onto earthenware. It was a cheaper alternative when compared to more expensive transferware and still came in a variety of colours: reds, blues, greens and browns were some of the most common. Sometimes this technique was used in collaboration with other painted elements. It experienced a decline during the early twentieth century but later had a revival. We still make spongeware today—you probably have some in your kitchen cupboard. Spongeware can look very similar to spatterware, which is basically controlled splashing. Some sources consider them the same thing but I think they differ.

Sherds of this pottery are often found discoloured as people used the cups and bowls to hold a variety of contents. It was very popular in farmhouses in rural areas as the pots were easy to replace but had enough decoration not to seem plain.

That concludes all the main pottery I am going to talk about; so, now that you know almost all the types of pottery you could find on the River Thames' foreshore, let's zoom into one that I have found! I have this piece of pottery, which I believe is tin-glazed. The glazing is very blurred, but you can see a fishing scene. I have also found a lot of pottery with houses visible in the decoration. Whole scenes, like the fishing scene, can be found on pottery, especially the white and blue coloured pottery. They often have the most intricate designs,

Above left: Some pottery including the fishing scene fragment. (*E. Vaxby*)

Above right: A brightly coloured piece of pottery: blue and green. (*E. Vaxby*)

which is why they are my favourite to find! Sometimes these houses are stylised, other times very realistic. In this chapter we have seen how many different styles there are when painting pottery, so let's have a look at glass next.

12

A Glance at Glass

Glass is partly made from sand and grinds down into something like sand too. Without knowing it, you've been stepping on tons of tiny pieces of glass every time you go to the foreshore. But, this glass is coming from somewhere: our treasures! As the years go on, the fragments of glass rolling at the bottom of the riverbed will get smaller and smaller, which is why it is so rare to find complete pieces.

Glass (and sea glass) is another of my all-time favourite finds. Glass from the foreshore comes in a range of colours, each shard looking like a gem. Different colours were popular in different periods of time and used for different things. For example, greens are most common with the common beer-bottle green we still see so much of today. But, there are also olives and aquas hiding by the rocks. One of my absolute favourite pieces is this olive-coloured sphere of glass. It isn't perfect in shape, with many bumps where the rocks have bruised its surface, but when you hold it against the light it is beautiful! Some of the rarest colours include purples and other blues. I have also found quite a few milk-glass shards which are opaque. This type of glass can often get confused with porcelain, especially at first glance, but you will find the sides of the gloss much smoother since it is not from a broken clay body. Finally, lettering on glass is quite common too.

Above left: Some iridescent glass and normal glass found at various locations by the River Thames, London. (*E. Vaxby*)

Above right: A clear frosted piece of glass with the letters 'N' and 's' on it. (*E. Vaxby*)

Now you have an idea of some of the glass you may find, let's have a look at each colour individually starting with the lightest: white glass (also known as clear glass). Clear glass was and still is used in all sorts of ways, from windows to drinking vessels. But when glass is tossed between the rocks in the river, you can get this beautiful frosted look. Sea glass is also sometimes named 'Mermaid's Tears' because tales say that when a captain died at sea, a mermaid who was in love with him cried, forming sea glass. A sad, yet beautiful story.

This process of making glass look frosted can happen over decades, even centuries, slowly wearing away at the glass' surface. This is what makes clear glass look white. You may think that white glass just encompasses one shade, but there are blue whites, yellow white, and even pink whites. When standing by themselves these shades all look white, but as soon as you put them together you can see the full range. When clear glass sits in the sun for years and years, it can change colour: from clear to the pinks and blues and yellows I was talking about. Temperature, ingredients, and what the glass has been exposed to in the outside world (like the sun) all play a role in the colour.

Though they have a bit of a peculiar name, Mermaid's Nipples are a special beach find and come from glass fishing floats and old bottle bases. Though we don't use glass floats much anymore, old broken ones from the sea still sometimes wash in the Thames, though you are more likely to find them while beachcombing on the coast. Fishing floats help show if there is a fish nibbling away at the fishing bait. The bottoms of old bottles (and the seals of the floats) are like little blobs, meaning they are slightly thicker than the other glass. This makes the rest of the bottle break off, but the mermaid's 'nipple' remains intact; they are so named because they are from the sea and are a whimsical shape. Most of the Mermaid's Nipples you will find here in the UK will have originally been part of a glass bottle.

Moving onto coloured glass, these fragments can come from anywhere and everywhere. Even stained-glass windows! Beginning with light aqua glass (yes, there are light and dark versions of the same colour with different uses!), this colour was used a lot in medicine bottles. Now that so many things come in plastic bottles, we don't see many of these aqua medicine bottles anymore, but there are thousands of fragments on the foreshore. Darker aqua is fancier, maybe used for glass art or expensive tableware. Both of these colours are very common in the Thames. I have found many, many pieces every time I have stepped onto the beach!

Next is blue glass. This was another colour used a lot for medicines—and poisons! Because it is so bright, it was meant to warn people to handle what was inside with caution. Sometimes even the words 'NOT TO BE TAKEN' can be found on the side of a bottle. But, in the nineteenth century many people were illiterate so could not read these signs which is why they used the brightly coloured glass; emerald green glass was another common colour for these poison bottles. However, blue glass was also popular for inkwells and perfume bottles.

Perfume bottles are very delicate, but I know mudlarks who have found whole ones on the foreshore. Old perfume and medicine bottles would have glass bottle stoppers which are often beautifully decorated. You will often only find one or the other, but if the stopper is strong enough (or maybe just stuck) and the river has been gentle with the bottle, you may just find the bottle and its bottle stopper together in the mud.

Most purple glass is clear glass from the nineteenth/twentieth century that has gone through the colour change process. But there are more modern purple glass fragments from things like glass art. Pink is another glass colour that can originally have been clear, but it was also used for decorative glass pieces like pink plates from the twentieth century.

Below left: Some glass: blues, greens, iridescent pieces, a bottle stopper, a clear frosted piece of glass with a 'B' in a diamond on it and some brown glass. (*E. Vaxby*)

Below right: The top of a brown-glass bottle still with its bottle stopper. (*E. Vaxby*)

Brown sea glass comes in a range of shades: from very light orangey-ambers to dark 'pirate' glass. It is another colour often used for beer bottles and other beverage bottles, and dark coloured glass is said to be stronger. The reason why so many beverage bottles for things like beer and wine are brown or a dark green is because these colours provide the best protection from daylight, therefore avoiding the alcohol developing an unappetising taste.

On the subject of pirate glass, this is a black-looking glass you can find quite a bit of on the Thames. But the name is misleading, as these pieces of glass will usually not have been held by a pirate. During the Golden Age of Piracy, rum was very popular and the dark colour of this glass was used to protect the liquid. On ships, many bottles were thrown overboard landing in the sea. Pirates were common in these times and wouldn't mind some rum, giving 'pirate' glass its nickname. However, if you hold this glass to a bright light (like the sun) you will see a colour like green or brown, sometimes even reds and blues! It is as if a pirate's treasure is being revealed. You can call it black glass because it looks so dark when lying on the foreshore, but it is actually just very dark coloured glass. Weathering, like the glass becoming frosted, can make the glass appear darker. Pirate glass can easily be mistaken for some pebbles on the beach, but these glass shards hold a secret light within! Next time you see a black-coloured piece of glass on the foreshore, hold it up to the light and see what colour it really is!

Red, orange and yellow are some of the other rare colours of sea glass, while canary glass is rare and a little dangerous. Canary glass, also known as Vaseline glass, is a yellow-green colour. Lots of fragments from tableware can be found on the foreshore from around the mid-1800s. However, uranium is an important ingredient in the glass. It gives the glass the bright green colour when in normal lighting and shows up as a glowing neon green under ultra violet light. Uranium is radioactive so when handling uranium glass you should do so with caution. From what I have heard, it is typically fine to touch the glass through casual contact but you should avoid

Right: A piece of bright green glass. (*E. Vaxby*)

Below: A picture taken on the Thames Path of Canary Wharf and other buildings. The foreshore near here (Stepney Beach) has lots of good glass. (*E. Vaxby*)

drinking or eating from it; however that is usually the case with everything from the Thames.

It is quite rare to find complete bottles on the Thames. I have found a few though they usually look as if they have not spent so long in the Thames. Beer bottles are the most common, while onion bottles are the rarest.

Onion bottles were a popular storage option for wine between the late seventeenth century and mid-eighteenth century. They are called onion bottles as their shape resembles an onion! The wide base made the bottle more stable than some other shapes at the time and helped ensure the safety of the liquid inside while sailing across stormy seas. Fragments of these green-glass bottles can be found along the Thames and if you find a whole one, you have every mudlark's dream in your hands. I have discovered a couple of bases which I believe are from onion bottles, though there is a small chance they are from some other glass vessel as I don't have the rest of the bottle. The bases I have found have some iridescence, which happens when alkali is leached out by the Thames' slightly acidic water. This then creates a very thin flaking glass that produces a rainbow effect when light travels though it. I have found some

Two glass bottle bases. (*E. Vaxby*)

Above left: A close-up on some iridescent shards of glass. (*E. Vaxby*)

Above right: Five iridescent fragments of glass on a piece of slate. (*E. Vaxby*)

other iridescent glass in the past but it isn't as common as you might think. You must be very gentle when handling iridescent glass as the surface can just flake off.

Marbles are rolling gems from a rolling river and often made of glass. I have found a few marbles before but they are often hard to date, just like other glass. The common glass marbles children still play with today were mass-produced, originally in Germany, in the mid-1800s . These marbles come in different colours and sizes and could easily continue to be used, though they are often slightly misshapen. You can also find spray-can marbles, which are a little less interesting to look at. They are used to mix up the paint inside of a spray can when you shake it, so when the can somehow ends up in the river and breaks, the marble turns up on the foreshore!

Two marbles found in Duinbergen in Belgium on a sandy beach. Their origin is most likely a modern children's game. (*E. Vaxby*)

In the nineteenth century, the Victorians were developing lots of new carbonated drinks. To prevent the carbonation from escaping the bottle, a soft-drink maker called Hiram Codd created a new glass bottle design. It had a glass marble and rubber washer inside the chamber in the bottle neck. With the pressure from the beverage's carbonation, the marble and washer created an air-tight seal meaning the fizziness would be retained. These Codd bottles, as they are named, are quite rare and I haven't found any yet myself—but the marbles are gems too! Children would break the bottles just to get to the marble inside. Though normal marbles are more aesthetically pleasing, these little balls of glass gave children something fun to play with in their free time. A little while later a new bottle design to preserve fizzy drinks was created, called torpedo bottles (because of their shape) they didn't have the fun marbles you could play with.

Glass buttons are also little treasures, just like marbles. They were very popular from the 1800s onwards and come in many different designs. Sometimes they are a flower or some sort of spiral, and sometimes they are just a plain piece of glass—but still beautiful! Glass buttons are quite rare, as are glass beads. Glass beads have been around for thousands of years; the Celts had them and Roman women wore them around their neck. These beads would have been smooth and shiny in the sunlight, but are now frosty and rough from the harsh conditions in the water. Trade beads can also be found and are quite beautiful—especially the Venetian ones! These Italian glassmakers produced some of the nicest trade beads around the 1600s. The beads from broken rosaries are also on the foreshore.

You can find quite a bit of hand-blown glass on the Thames' foreshore. It is often quite difficult to find the origin of glass, but just like with pottery, letters can be found on glass giving us hints—

Below left: A small piece of light green glass found in Wapping held up to the light. (*E. Vaxby*)

Below right: The small piece of green glass photographed in situ. (*E. Vaxby*)

Above left: A sharp fragment of a dark teal coloured piece of glass. Found on Wapping Beach. (*E. Vaxby*)

Above right: The bottom of a brown beer bottle made of glass. (*E. Vaxby*)

maybe even answers—to where the glass is from. Sometimes the unique colours that you have never seen before were made with someone's bare hands. Other times, something simply went wrong in the factory.

Bottle seals often include some of this information. The seal is thicker than the bottle so as the bottle breaks, the seal stays in one piece. These seals were used to personalise wine bottles. If you do a bit of digging in antique bottle books, you might find out who owned the bottle seal and their whole backstory! The wealthy often used bottle seals to personalise their bottles and they were a symbol of status.

With lettering on glass, sometimes it wears away due to all of the tossing and tumbling in the river. However, on one of my trips down to the river, I spotted a clear piece of glass with the word MILK on it. Before our modern milk cartons, we had milk bottles which I presume is the origin of this piece of glass.

Multicoloured glass is also a thing—it is not as common as the single colours but still a relatively normal find on the foreshore. In my opinion, the hardest glass to find on the foreshore is milk or opaque glass.

In July 2025, I found a piece of glass with the sticker still attached. Usually stickers rub off in the water but this plastic film was holding two pieces of the glass together. I thought I would take a picture as it had 'roll rock' written on it. I wasn't sure where it was from at the time, but I have now learnt that Rolling Rock is a beer brand. It is still being brewed and sold, and available in the UK. The company started in 1939 by the Tito Brothers who owned the

Below left: A piece of green glass with a sticker on it saying 'roll rock' found on the North bank of the River Thames. (*E. Vaxby*)

Below right: A piece of wired glass. (*E. Vaxby*)

Latrobe Brewery. I didn't end up taking this piece home, but it was fun to research the story behind it.

There is also a lot of wired glass by the Thames, a type of glass with a metal grid inside. Though you have to be careful when picking this up because the metal rods can be poking out. It is primarily used for its fire resistant properties.

The River Thames view from the foreshore. (*E. Vaxby*)

13

Pipes from the Past

On to clay pipes—a topic that can be broken into two pieces: the pipe stems and the pipe bulbs.

But let's start by looking at the whole thing.

Clay pipes have been around in England for about 500 years. Their shape has changed over time, with the first pipe bowls being very small and the later ones from the eighteenth century having enough space to fit my thumb! At first, only the wealthy could smoke these tobacco pipes but as more tobacco was imported into England it caused the price to drop. These tobacco pipes could be very long—the longest were between 12 and 26 inches long! Almost all of the pipes are broken now, but if you are lucky there is a chance you uncover a complete pipe buried in the dense, anaerobic mud. They were only used once (until the tobacco was finished) and often thrown into the Thames.

London itself is built on London Clay, or at least most of it. It is excellent at preserving things like fossils, but it is all hidden beneath the city. The Thames flows over the 'London Basin' which is chalk, sand, gravel and clay. The area which is called the London Basin has a varied topography; it has a chalk basis with gravel and clay on top, but the depth of the chalk layer varies depending on the location.

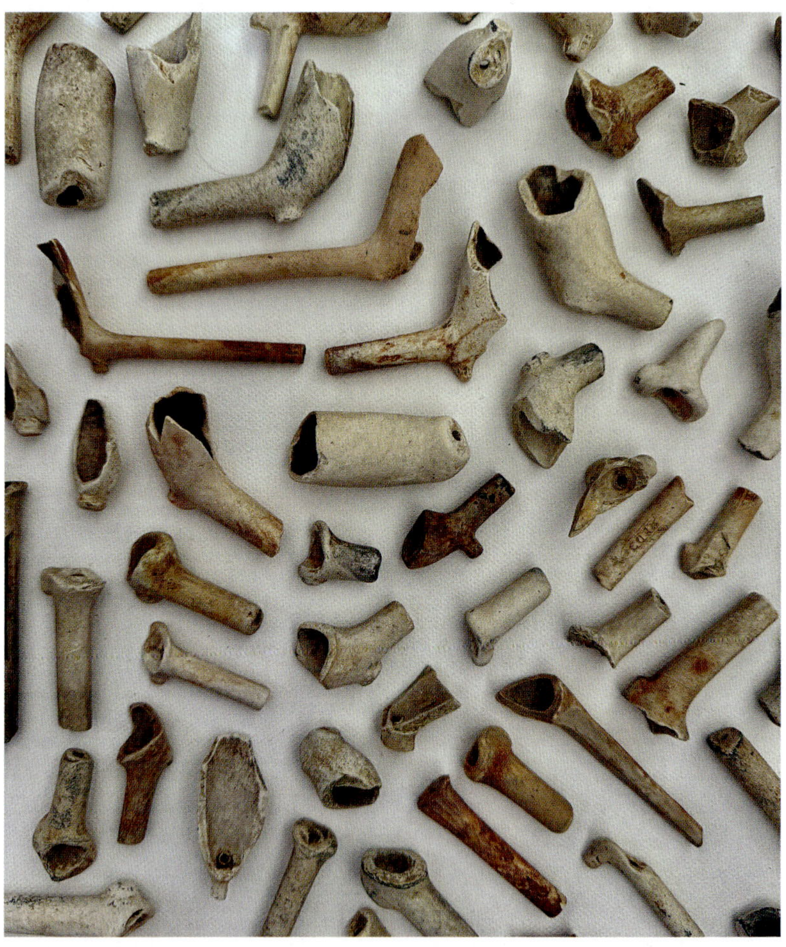

Lots of clay pipe fragments, bowls and stems. (*E. Vaxby*)

The Thames may look dirty, but it is actually just carrying silt and other sediments. Now I am not saying you should go and drink this water, as there have been many nasty sewage spills in there, however its colour is not primarily from pollution. The pollution problem in the Thames is still an important issue that we need to properly

Right: A close up of lots of pipe stem fragments. (*E. Vaxby*)

Below: A wave hitting the stony foreshore at Wapping. (*E. Vaxby*)

address, but it isn't the major reason why the Thames is a yucky brown. You might also sometimes find some algae on your finds but that can all be scrubbed off.

Pipe bulbs have many different designs—and I am not just talking about their shape. Pipe makers (whose makers' marks can sometimes be found on the foot of the bulb) used moulds to perfect the pipe's design. Whole scenes can be found on the bulbs with decoration to the end of the stem. Sometimes you might find a dog perched between the bulb and the stem. Or maybe, a pattern running from the rim down to the foot. The foot of a pipe is the part just beneath the bowl. At first it had a functional use: to allow the clay pipe to stand upright. Later on it became smaller and smaller, transforming into a decorative element.

Other common designs include symbols to do with the military, such as coats of arms and flags. These can be quite rare but carry a lot of information about the past consumer. Finally, Turk's head pipe bowls are a common feature on the clay pipes. The first coffee shop opened in 1652 with coffee imported from Turkey. The illustration of a Turk's head was often used as an advertisement for the coffee shops. Drinking this beverage and smoking clay pipes was a very common way to spend your free time during the eighteenth and nineteenth centuries. And that is why so many pipe bowls are decorated with a Turk's head (the face of a man wearing a turban). This design has many variations, but always has the face pointing away from the smoker.

To clarify things, the bowl of the pipe is the bulb at the end of a long, thin, stem-like cylinder. The foreshore is littered with hundreds of broken pipe stems: if you tried to take them all, you would be stuck there for days! The foot of the pipe bulb is not on all of the clay pipe shapes; some don't have feet while others do. Think of these pipes as modern cigarettes.

The maker's mark I mentioned before was often just the initials of the creator on the foot of the bulb. Sometimes you will also find a stamp on the bulb though the one I found was quite weathered.

Above left: A display of broken pipe bulbs and pipe stems. (*E. Vaxby*)

Above right: Lots of pipe stem fragments in a glass jar, sealed with a cork. (*E. Vaxby*)

I managed to make out a human figure but it could easily be a horse too!

The stems of pipes come in a variety of different sizes as they tend to get smaller as the stem goes on. I have found pipe stems which would have snapped if I picked them up with too much force. On the other hand, I have also seen pipe stems that were thicker than a pencil!

I remember finding my first few pipe bulbs; I was at Limehouse mudlarking on quite a pebbly beach, not much mud around at all. I had done all of my treasure hunting on the main beach and decided to go exploring on this little stretch of land which was almost always covered by the tide. Today, the tide was low enough to go have a look. I walked over there and started looking for the usuals: pottery, glass and pipe stems. What I saw next was the best surprise you could get for a young mudlark—a pipe bulb! I had been watching Nicola White's videos on YouTube for quite a while and had seen all of the wonderful pipes she pulls out of the mud. I wasn't expecting this pipe to just be lying there. I picked it up and ran over to tell my parents. I couldn't believe it! After taking a photo to put on my blog, I went to check out if by chance there were more pipes around that area. I had never seen anyone mudlark there before as it can be accessed only for around half an hour each low-tide. The river decided it was my lucky day and gave me five bulbs in total. Three of them are proper pipe bulbs with a good chunk of the pipe stem still attached. The other two were just the edge of the bulb and some stem but I am still grateful to have found them.

A collection of bits of pipe. (*E. Vaxby*)

A broken pipe bulb found on Bankside, photographed in situ. (*E. Vaxby*)

Since then I have found numerous more pipe bulbs, most coming from between 1750 and 1860. I believe that the first pipe bulb I found was from the 1820–60s. Online guides will help you to tell what time period a pipe bulb is from, but you will get used to recognising the shapes after a while; as I mentioned before, the earlier pipe bulbs are much smaller than the later ones. A couple of mine have some ridges around the rim to add decoration. The first pipes that were made in the sixteenth and seventeenth centuries lacked decorations—they were simple and plain. Pipe makers started using moulds in the mid-eighteenth century to add aesthetic appeal. Stamps were also used to add decoration or information about the pipe.

Finding pipe bulbs can be hard. Shapes on the foreshore sometimes deceive you; when you go to have a look, it is only a rock. When in mud, you might only see the stem poking out of the surface. Give it a gentle tug. If it comes right out, you may only have one end. If it is a little stubborn, you will have to do some pipe extracting. A mudlark's favourite! If you have a trowel, you can slowly dig around the pipe, dislodging mud. If you don't have one yet—your fingers will do! Once you have removed enough mud around the clay pipe, you will hopefully be able to pull it out of the mud without breaking it. And that, ladies and gentlemen, is how you extract a pipe bulb.

There is also The Society for Clay Pipe Research, which I learnt about at a mudlarking talk. They have documents with many pipe makers' initials on them so that you can identify the pipe maker and learn about their life. The National Pipe Archive also has lots of good resources to help you date your pipe, clean them and more. From this I found out about William Manby.

I have a pipe stem with the start of the bowl, and on the foot the letters W and M are embossed on each side, with a crown. I was looking through some mudlarking posts one day and came across a picture of a pipe stem and foot from a fellow mudlark that looked almost exactly the same to the one I had lying at home. I had first thought that the symbol above the letters was an anchor, but it turns out that the sides had just worn away and it is in fact a crown. I then did a little bit of researching and found some sites relating these initials and the crown to the pipe maker William Manby of Limehouse. I went to find another source because fact-checking is always important and discovered a publication on The National Pipe Archive.[1]

1. Higgins, D. A., 2004, 'Appendix 2: The Clay Tobacco Pipes', in G. Keevill, *The Tower of London Moat: Archaeological Excavations 1995–9*, Historic Royal Palaces Monograph No. 1 (published by Oxford Archaeology, Oxford), pp. 241–270 (315pp).

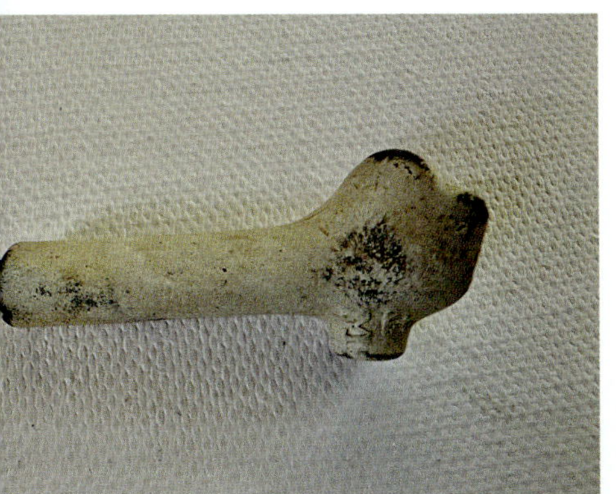

Above left: The foot of a pipe bulb, created by William Manby. The maker's mark here is an 'M' with a crown. (*E. Vaxby*)

Above right: The other side of the William Manby fragment, featuring a 'W' and a crown. (*E. Vaxby*)

It said that the Manbys were prominent pipemakers and William Manby specifically was working between 1719 and 1763. Several of these pipes have been found but usually not a whole! I also found a publication by Jacqui Pearce in the archive about the clay pipes produced by the Manby family which was very interesting to read. Through just two letters and a symbol on a piece of clay, I managed to uncover William Manby's life story and everything that went along with it! It appears he had a son called Richard who was also into pipemaking. This Richard also had a son called Richard (again), which sometimes makes reading academic papers a little confusing! In some papers there is talk about there being multiple Williams in the Manby family too but I have only seen that information once.

From the piece of writing by Jacqui Pearce, we learn that Manby gave his address as Green Dragon Alley at some point. This alley no longer exists but from what I have read on different sites, it may have gone from modern day Garnet Street to somewhere around

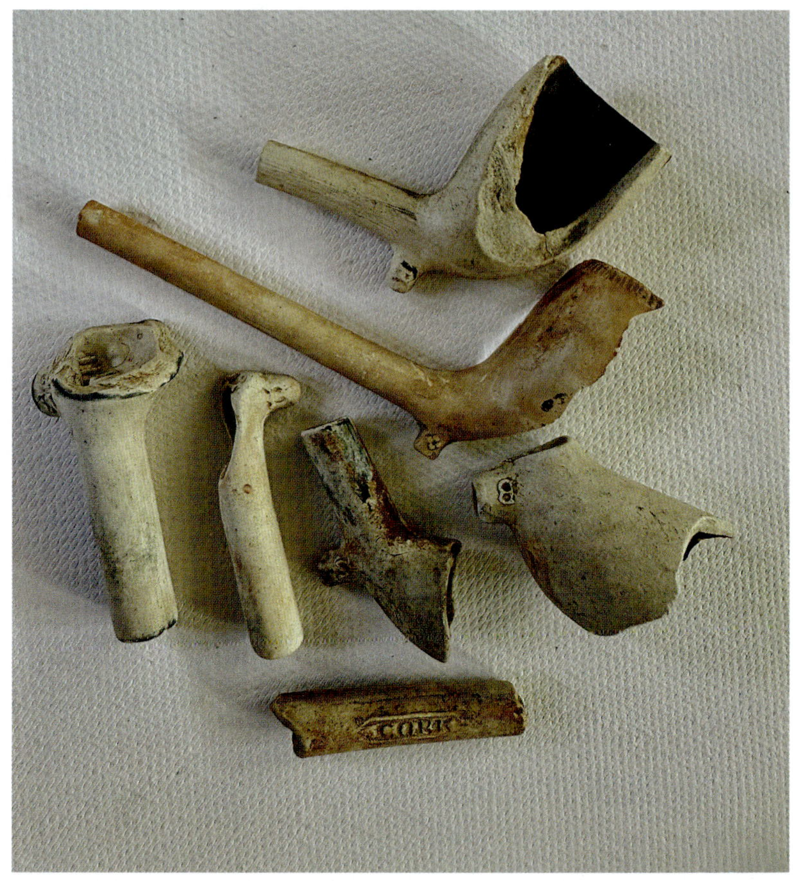

An arrangement of precious pipes, including William Manby's. (*E. Vaxby*)

the spot where Glamis Road crosses the entrance to Shadwell Basin. This is actually all in my local area, so it is interesting to see how this pipe didn't travel very far. I don't remember whether I found it in Wapping or Limehouse, but the river could easily have carried it a couple hundred metres. Maybe William Manby smoked the pipe himself!

14

Mysterious Treasures

You have almost all of the knowledge nailed down now. Pottery, pipe bulbs, glass. Now, you just need to uncover the mysteries.

For a while now, mudlarks have been finding garnets on the Thames. These semi-precious gems are just lying on the foreshore, sometimes in whole clusters together. They glitter in the sunlight as the water swashes around them. Garnets are a strong red colour and are used a lot in rings and other jewellery. They are mysterious though because, how did they get there?

Mudlarks and historians alike have been pondering this and many theories have been hypothesised but not much is known for certain. From my research, I have learnt that garnets are not native to the Thames, meaning they don't belong there naturally, but have been deposited there. But by whom? And why?! Some believe that they were lost unintentionally while on the way to a jewellers before the Thames swallowed them up. This is the only plausible theory I have found, but there aren't any records I could access indicating whether this could be true.

Some mudlarks have collections of hundreds of garnets from the Thames, but they only appear in certain spots. Being a mudlark is the same as being a detective. We have to use multiple sources and the help of others to figure out the truth behind every case. But this case, which has been tried and tested, is still left unsolved.

Above left: A very muddy Wapping foreshore, with my pink boots in frame. (*E. Vaxby*)

Above right: A pottery fragment found by another mudlark in Wapping which reads '& Co, King's Cross, N.' around the edge. (*E. Vaxby*)

I mentioned how you can clean rusty padlocks earlier in the book, but you don't know much about them yet. Padlocks have been around since Roman times but most of what you will find on the foreshore is from more modern times. Padlocks have been used to prevent theft of belongings for centuries. Sometimes, one might malfunction and end up in the Thames. You can also find love padlocks. London has many walls where couples will put a padlock to symbolise their eternal love. The best quality padlocks cost a lot so the average padlock on those walls might not last very long. But, we don't always know where a padlock comes from. And where is the key? Does it possibly have a code and can you crack it? I have found many padlocks on the Thames foreshore, though most of them have such a thick layer of crust I prefer to leave them there.

There are also a lot of signs on the river. From little labels to whole street signs. 'DO NOT TRESPASS' is a common one to find. These probably just fell off and ended up in the river but when you find little things with inscriptions on them, there can be a much bigger story. For example, you might find something with a name. The internet is filled with people from the past so you are quite likely to find something about them on there, even if it is just a snippet of history. If it has a business name on it like XYZ hotel or an address, the search bar is your friend. Once when I had a Meet the Mudlark event, one of the mudlarks who came found a piece of pottery which read '& Co,' on the top and 'King's Cross, N.' on the bottom. I didn't find much about it online but it could be from a restaurant in that area. How it got into the Thames—your guess is as good as mine.

At that Mudlark with Me, I also came across a piece of pottery just as we were wrapping up for the day. After inspecting it a little closer, it looks like there are five white sheep and one black one on a fence-line field with trees. Google didn't give me much, but it looks like the shard is tin-glazed. For the moment I have come to a dead end, but I might stumble across the answer in the future!

A sherd of pottery featuring a pasture lined by a fence, with sheep on it. Found in Wapping. (*E. Vaxby*)

When documenting your finds, you can either take photos or write them down in a log book. Maybe both! If you have some time on your hands, you could even make a sketch of your treasure. That seems fitting, considering that artists have made almost everything we find on the foreshore. But we all lose things sometimes—I have lost many paintbrushes. They probably end up in the same place as hairbands and left socks, right? Well, paint pans like those you find in your watercolour box are actually quite common to find on the foreshore but you have to have a good eye to spot them though as otherwise they disappear among the rocks.

A mystery that was only unearthed recently was the 500-year-old 'booted man'. Archaeologists working for the Museum of London Archaeology—also known as MOLA—uncovered a skeleton of a man face down in the mud wearing knee-high leather boots. He had

The rocky foreshore near Wapping Wall in East London. (*E. Vaxby*)

one arm above his head and the other arm bent to the side. This was near Tower Bridge at one of the sites being used to build the new Thames Tideway Tunnel (for sewage). Experts discovered grooves in his teeth which, if he was a sailor, could have been from repeatedly holding the rope in his mouth. What his occupation had been is unclear, but he may have died on the job while on or by the river. How did he get to the foreshore, and why was he wearing such high boots? He could have fallen or drowned, maybe stuck in the mud.

View of Tower Bridge. (*E. Vaxby*)

Specialists believe that the boots date all the way back to around the early sixteenth century. They could have been used as waders.

There are a lot of pewter toys found when mudlarking, along with lead ones too. Pewter was used to make toys for children in the medieval period! That was a good couple of years ago. Toy knights, figurines of people and animals were all common. Just like parents today, medieval parents were also devoted to their children, wanting them to have as much luxury as possible. This came in the form of toys.

Nymphs have been part of the Thames for a long time, or so they say. Memorials for them are along the river. For instance, the nymph that was once by Somerset House, and now in Bushy Park. This statue is more commonly known as the Diana Fountain. By definition, a nymph is a mythological spirit resembling a pretty maiden. Nymphs are said to inhabit places such as rivers and woods. Do you think there were ever nymphs in the Thames? Now there's another mystery for you to solve.

A view of the Millenium Footbridge from Bankside, with St Paul's Cathedral in the background of the image. (*E. Vaxby*)

15

Conclusion

That's a wrap! You are in the know with the mudlarking community now! You are kitted up with the right gear ready to take a leap onto the foreshore by the locations you have carefully picked out. You have your list of things you want to find: onion bottles, pipe bulbs, Roman coins etc. All you need now is the permit you have applied for, so that you can legally mudlark.

My usual lark will be about forty-five minutes to two hours long. It depends what time I arrived at my location. Some beaches can be accessed for much longer periods of time while others are only there for a moment. I don't go night-larking much but treasure hunting in the evening when the clouds start to go pink and the evening breeze glides through the air is always relaxing. After I have come down the slippery steps, I tread carefully along the foreshore.

Before going mudlarking, I will probably have some ideas of what I want to find that day. It is usually a mix of pottery, glass and pipe bulbs, but it depends on what I found last time. My rubber boots are good for keeping my feet dry but mudlarking in the rain can get quite cold. The sun needs to be out for a fun day for me. Of course, if you live in London you don't really have a say in whether the skies are blue ,as most of the time the clouds decide to roll in

Above left: A fragment of pottery found at Stepney Beach. (*E. Vaxby*)

Above right: A common Southwater Brick, made in Sussex. Found by the wooden structures in Wapping. (*E. Vaxby*)

Below left: Teeth from Stepney Beach. (*E. Vaxby*)

Below right: Small teeth from the foreshore near Limehouse. (*E. Vaxby*)

so sometimes I have to compromise. I love mudlarking in autumn and spring because you don't sizzle in the heat or freeze in the cold.

Back to my mudlarking adventures, when I am nearing the end of my trip to the foreshore, I usually lay out all of my finds and see my haul. Sometimes I come across something in my bag that I don't even remember finding! I then take a picture so I know what I mudlarked, where and when and I usually share it online so that other mudlarks can see what's in the area!

Wapping Beach, with Canary Wharf in the background. (*E. Vaxby*)

This book is just one of many that can get you started in the mudlarking world. Mudlarks Lara Maiklem and Jason Sandy have also written books which I have learnt a lot from. They also share lots of valuable information on their social media. Nicola White's YouTube channel is also a valuable source of information that I warmly recommend. Then if you just want some friends to help you along the way, you could also share your finds online like Jason or Lara do, because peoples' comments often give you leads to where a find could be from. More experienced mudlarks are always happy to help those beginning their life on the foreshore. Mudlarking talks and exhibitions are very popular in London, with many to choose from. I definitely recommend the one in Southwark Cathedral if it is still around when you read this!

A paw print in the sand on the foreshore. (*E. Vaxby*)

The future of mudlarking is mysterious yet bright. Will it become more popular and the whole of London starts scavenging the shores of the Thames? Or will the secret foreshore club remain hidden from the rest of the city for a while longer. The waitlist for a permit is very long, with only a few spots opening every now and again. The reporting obligations are also becoming stricter. But these restrictions make sure no items of value are lost or forgotten. All history is important and we need to make sure it is safe by recording what we find. Whether that is in a journal, on a blog or (for more valuable finds) to the Finds Liaison Officer at the Portable Antiquities Scheme. Remember, the whole foreshore is an archaeological site, changing twice a day with new discoveries to be made. With the permits, it also means that the people mudlarking on the Thames are aware of the dangers that come with the river. The foreshore itself is also changing; with more clippers going up and down and new sewage systems being added, some of our spots might disappear or lose their special touch. That being said, something might have been stirred up from the very depths of the river and is now lying somewhere on the banks just waiting to be discovered by a mudlark.

The riverside beaches are used for other reasons too. Not just mudlarking. I have seen people picnic here and sunbathe in the summer—there are even sometimes parties, though I doubt these are always legal.... Back in time, in the 1950s, the foreshore was used as a makeshift seaside beach for those without the means to travel to the coast. The poor East End families travelled to spots like Tower Beach which is very sandy. Tower Beach was located outside of the Tower of London near Tower Bridge. This was an artificial beach opened by King George V in July of 1934. It was made by importing sand and then dumping it by the riverbank. Thousands of people visited it up until it closed in 1971. There were attempts to reopen the beach, such as the campaign 'Reclaim the Beach'. The beach was nicknamed 'London's Riviera'. You could take a dip in the water, rent little boats and relax on the sandy beach.

I believe mudlarking will never lose its magic. The feeling when you find something meaningful is truly special and I hope you will get to experience it! The excitement when you see a pipe bulb poking out of the mud, or the exhilaration when you see a button hiding by a rock!

A lovely rock found in Wapping. (*E. Vaxby*)

Epilogue

My Latest Mudlark

It was the day before I left for summer camp. I wanted to get another mudlark in before we went abroad. See the Thames one last time.

My mother and I were going to mudlark by the Tate. We had taken the DLR to Bank Station and then walked from there. The steps were very slippery; it had been raining just moments before! The moist smell that comes after rain was still hanging in the air, mixing with the strong scent of caramelised peanuts coming from the nearby bridges. But now the skies had opened up once more and drowned the city in sunlight. A rare occurrence in London! As I looked above me, a flock of seagulls swept over our heads.

On this mudlarking trip I was hoping to find some sherds of blue pottery. I hadn't been mudlarking much here before, maybe once or twice a while ago, so I wasn't sure what to expect. But there were bones everywhere, along with many covered pipe stems. And then I saw it, my first find of the day! It was a beautiful piece of tin-glazed stoneware. I recognised it as soon as I saw it. I have learnt a lot of things about mudlarking in the past few years and it does come in handy! I bet if I had seen this a year or two prior to this mudlark, I wouldn't have been able to identify the specifics of this ceramic fragment.

Some shouts were coming from the streets, reminding me that I was still in busy London. The tide was on its way up so I had

Above: Very muddy steps which are a slipping hazard. (*E. Vaxby*)

Left: A picture from my most recent mudlark of the foreshore, with the Thames in sight. (*E. Vaxby*)

limited time to find my treasures. There were many other mudlarks on the beach that day, presumably because of the nice afternoon weather. The foreshore had been pecked clean of everything else so we decided to head over the bridge to go mudlark outside the art gallery. This part was sandier than the foreshore across the river. I continued mudlarking for another half-an-hour before my mother and I headed over to a cafe. I looked into my treasure bag while we were walking. I had quite a selection of finds: pipe stems, aqua sea glass, a Willow Pattern fragment and a knife handle. There had been some more glass on the beach but my bag had gotten very heavy so I decided to leave them for another mudlark. I was very excited about researching what I had found when I got home. There was a new design on one of the pieces of pottery I hadn't seen before. It had blue and white glazing like most of the other pottery I had found that day, but the style was much more fluid and felt less planned. I guess I still had a lot to learn about all the different designs out there!

Now that I know so much more about mudlarking than I did at the beginning of my digging journey, it is easier to tell whether an object is trash or treasure, since I know how common things are on the foreshore. You could say I have trained my eye from all my practice. I get very excited when I spot something rare, but love my frequent finds too. I usually look for something specific, whether glass, pottery or pipe bulbs. I am still looking for some more unique pipe bowls and I am hoping I will discover some in my upcoming mudlarks. I am always looking for special finds, but my favourite

Right: Some treasures from my most recent mudlark by the Thames Beach. (*E. Vaxby*)

Below: A pottery sherd found in East London. (*E. Vaxby*)

Above left: A piece of blue and white coloured ceramic found in Wapping. (*E. Vaxby*)

Above right: The foreshore, an image taken from above. (*E. Vaxby*)

treasure is always coming across a piece of blue and white coloured pottery. I'm not sure why, but it has just been like that since the beginning. My collection of these sherds is probably double the size of my other pottery.

When you are just beginning, it can get frustrating when the river hasn't stirred up what you are looking for. A feeling of urgency washes over you whenever you mudlark, with the tide threatening to steal all of its treasures back. Mudlarking needs knowledge and patience, but also quite a bit of luck. But once you get into the mudlarking zone, you will soon find that your treasure bag is almost full. After every mudlark, I always feel happy: mudlarking is a real mood-booster! It has always been a happy place for me.

So to the Thames we will go! Peter Ackroyd puts it nicely in *Thames: Sacred River*:

> [The Thames] is patient, making its way through every obstacle. It is ruthless, wearing down the hardest rocks. It is unpredictable, especially when the current is interrupted or diverted. Its course from source to sea has been categorised as one of youth, maturity and old age. Its character changes within each terrain.

We often personify the river, letting Old Father Thames tell us his stories. It is like a friendly companion, speaking to you in soft whispers and splashes. I enjoy the tranquillity on the foreshore; the sense of the sea just out of arm's reach. On windy days you can almost smell the salt. No matter if you are mudlarking for only a moment or for the entirety of the low tide, the time on the foreshore will leave you inspired.

I am sure you will find some wonderful treasures! Beginner's luck is a good thing on the foreshore.

From one mudlark to another,

Emmylou

Acknowledgements

Well, that is the book—I spent a lot of time writing it and researching all of the facts. Most of it came from what I already have in my head but I dug a little deeper into the internet's mud to find the rest. Jason Sandy's book *Mudlarks: Treasures from the Thames*, and *Beachcombing Magazine*'s articles also proved excellent sources. Most of my summer was spent playing hockey or spending time with friends and family on the Belgian coast followed by me typing away on my laptop. But, before you get to the other cover, I would like to thank some people who have played a vital role in bringing this book to life.

First, my parents, who helped take my author photos and pick out topics that they would find interesting in a mudlarking book. Then, of course, my best friends. ODN was there from the beginning, receiving a very excited phone call from me after school one day. I had gotten an e-mail about the idea of this book while on the train home from school and as soon as I had told my parents her phone rang! AD has also always supported my mudlarking, coming to my events or supporting my small business. Then I think MM was the biggest help, even though we were spending the summer in different countries on opposite sides of the planet, she made sure that I wrote a little bit everyday by sending me lots of motivational messages! Then my little brother Edgar for always coming to all my book things even though I think he would

Right: A leaf lying on rocks, seen at Wapping Beach. (*E. Vaxby*)

Below: An image of me and my little brother on the foreshore back in 2020. (*E. Vaxby*)

have rather played football. I also wanted to thank RH and CW as they started it all! CW took me and RH down to the foreshore years ago, and those treasures are still safely stored at home. Then some of the stars of the show behind the scenes were all of the people at Fonthill Media Publishing for making this book come to life! Without this opportunity, this book would be nothing more than one very, very long Word document! I would like to especially thank Jay Slater for all of his hard work on this book and giving me the opportunity at the beginning.

Then I want to thank Nicola White for her lovely foreword to this book. She is the inspiration that started my whole mudlarking journey. I have been following her videos ever since I watched my first one back in 2020. Wow, that seems like a long time ago! But I have been learning ever since! I would also like to thank Anja Lanin for all the trips to Folkestone.

Below left: Myself, Edgar and my father on the Thames many years ago. (*C. Kontz*)

Below right: An image of Edgar and myself many years ago mudlarking. (*C. Kontz*)

A picture of my father, myself and my brother walking back up the foreshore. (*C. Kontz*)

Finally, I would like to thank my primary school teachers. Ms Jones and Ms Schindler probably saw a lot of grammatical errors but if they had not been corrected, this document would have many squiggly red underlines. Mr Browne supported my passion for the environment. Ms Khan was also there helping even earlier—in my third year in school I joined an afterschool club with her where we wrote our own book. Though mine only had about 100 words and was about famous TV characters, you could say it laid my foundations as a writer. I still have the book at home, the pages holding together with Sellotape. Last but not least, my two headmasters have supported me in all my endeavours. Mr S. Larter-Evans throughout primary school and Mr R. Tillett at my secondary school.

But, of course, I have forgotten someone. And he is the most important of them all: Old Father Thames. Without the river, there would be no mudlarking for me to write about. Maybe historic bits and bobs but none of the best stuff!

But thank you too, the readers! You are almost at the end of the book. Your sail from the Thameshead to the North Sea is almost finished. Where will you go next? Maybe back to the foreshore, where I wish you all of the best luck on your mudlarking adventures!

Above left: Nicola White interviewing me at my clean-up in Wapping a couple of years ago. (*C. Kontz/E. Vaxby*)

Above right: The opposite bank of the River Thames, as seen from Limehouse. (*E. Vaxby*)

Below: The foreshore at Wapping on a partly cloudy day. (*E. Vaxby*)

Glossary

Accretion: The gradual build-up of sediments along the shores. Sediment accretion does occur on the Thames particularly in marshland areas and the tidal estuary. Accretion can bury artifacts, protecting them under the riverbed for centuries. Finds like leather shoes and textiles owe their survival in the Thames to the thick layers that accumulated over the years above them.

Anaerobic mud: An environment where there is little to no oxygen, making the Thames mud perfect for preserving things. The very low oxygen levels prevent the usual decay processes. The Thames is famous for having these conditions as the mud preserves many organic materials such as wood, rope and leather. For example, leather Tudor shoes have survived ages in this anaerobic mud—Chapter 10.

Anchor: An anchor is used to secure a vessel in place on the water. They are heavy and often quite large. A very common material they are made of is metal. Mudlarks have found large anchors from ships before, but they often leave them on the foreshore as they are a very big and heavy find!

Bankside: Home to markets, Shakespeare's Globe and the Tate Modern, this side of the river Thames is full of life. It also has a rich history: this was the area for pleasure, away from the city life back in the day. Gambling houses, theatres, pubs and bear-baiting

Left: A muddy foreshore at Wapping. (*E. Vaxby*)

Below: Moored Boats seen in London on the River Thames. (*E. Vaxby*)

pits filled the streets. In the sixteenth century, activities like these were banned in the City of London. Southwark Cathedral, which was constructed in 1839, is also in this area. (Important Place Mentioned)—Chapter 5.

Barge: A type of flat-bottomed boat for carrying freight. Either towed or using its own power—Chapter 1.

Bartmann (Bellarmine) Jug: Also known as a witch bottle, these salt-glazed stoneware jugs originate from sixteenth-century Germany. They are famous for their decoration: the face of a bearded man on the neck of the bottle. In German, Bartmann means bearded man. They were originally used to store liquids, but during witch trials, people would put things that they believed would ward off evil spirits into these jugs—Chapter 1

Beachcombing: The act of searching along a beach looking for items of interest and/or value that have washed up or been left on the seashore. This activity has been around for hundreds of years and you can do it along many coastlines around the world—Chapter 1.

Right: The dunes in Flanders in the North of Belgium. Behind, the North Sea can be seen. (*E. Vaxby*)

Below: A cork found on a Belgian beach (top). (*E. Vaxby*)

Above left: A cork found on a Belgian beach (bottom). (*E. Vaxby*)

Above right: A cork found on a Belgian beach (side). (*E. Vaxby*)

Bermondsey: On the south bank of the Thames in the London Borough of Southwark. It is located just east of Tower Bridge. During the Industrial Revolution, Bermondsey was known for its tanneries and leatherworking. It was also nicknamed 'Biscuit Town' because of a company supplying biscuits for the French Army.

Billingsgate Fish Market: Back in the seventeenth century this fish market was open-air. It was around before then, but was not made official until 1698. Billingsgate Fish Market had boats deliver the fish and then business would be conducted on the riverside. A building was then designed and constructed, but the market later relocated to Poplar in East London. This was in 1982. The market is still alive, but the fish travel by road instead of ship.

Blackfriars: Located in central London, this area is named after the Dominican friars who wore black robes in the thirteenth century. During the sixteenth and seventeenth centuries, this was a printing hub with Fleet Street in this neighbourhood. The foreshore here has provided medieval finds.

Bottle stopper: A closure that fits into the neck of a bottle to seal the opening. Glass bottle stoppers started being widely used in the mid-nineteenth century—Chapter 5.

British Empire (time period: 1583–1997): The British Empire took many forms throughout the years, with Britain always at the centre. The empire started with the expansion overseas to the Americas. Fifty-six countries were directly under British rule at some point. At its peak, the empire was presided over by Queen Victoria, who reigned between 1837 and 1901. However, due to the impacts of two world wars and rebellions against British rule, which had also treated a lot of people very badly, the British Empire became smaller and smaller. However, the Commonwealth of Nations today still includes the majority of the fifty-six countries once under the umbrella of the British Empire.

A speed boat zooming along past me, with Canary Wharf in the background. (*E. Vaxby*)

Canary Wharf: From 1802 until the 1980s, the area we now associate with Canary Wharf was part of the Isle of Dogs and Poplar. It was one of the busiest docks in the world! The Canary Wharf we know today is a group of sky-rises for commercial, residential and business uses. (Important Place Mentioned)—Chapter 1.

Castaway: Someone who has been shipwrecked and stranded in an isolated place.

Causeway: A paved or cobbled path that leads down onto the foreshore to allow carts and horses and pedestrians alike to access the river at low tide. They are key features in the historic landscape of the Thames. Many old causeways have survived.

Cutter: A type of boat with a single mast and multiple headsails—Chapter 1.

Cutty Sark: A ship built in Scotland back in 1869. Now, it has stopped sailing around the world and has become a museum ship in Greenwich, London. While it was being restored, it suffered from a fire but did reopen in 2012. It brings visitors knowledge about maritime history. It is currently owned by the Royal Museums Greenwich. (Important Place Mentioned)—Chapter 5.

A causeway in Greenwich. (*E. Vaxby*)

Above left: Possibly the remnants of an old causeway. (*E. Vaxby*)

Above right: The *Cutty Sark* in Greenwich. (*E. Vaxby*)

Clay Pipe: A pipe used to smoke tobacco, made from hardened clay. These tobacco pipes were very popular between the sixteenth and nineteenth centuries, with their peak being around the 1700s—Chapter 3.

Codd bottle or a Codd-neck bottle: A type of glass bottle designed for carbonated drinks. It has a marble inside—Chapter 12.

Concretion: A hard crust of mineral deposits and silt that forms around objects buried in the mud. You can find it on iron objects like nails, spikes and tools. This extra layer can protect them from decay. Removing a concretion requires careful removal and conservation skills.

Cormorant: A large waterbird often seen diving for fish in the River Thames. Their lifespan is between six and eleven years, or longer.

Crab: A crustacean that can be found living in the Thames. The non-native Chinese Mitten Crabs are an invasive species and outcompete native crabs. You can sometimes see the remains of dead crabs on the foreshore beside the bones of forgotten animals.

Creamware: A clear lead-glazed earthenware with a cream-coloured body. Known in the Netherlands as '*Engels porselein*'

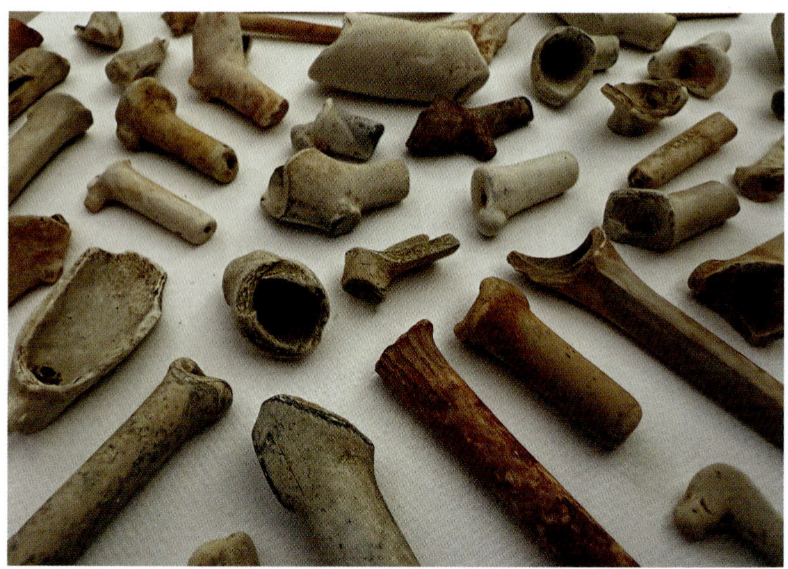

A selection of clay pipe bulbs and pipe stems (and pipe feet). (*E. Vaxby*)

(English porcelain), and in Italy as '*terraglia inglese*' (English earthenware)—Chapter 11.

Crockery: Plates, dishes, cups, and other similar items, especially ones made of earthenware or china.

Delftware: A Dutch type of tin-glazed pottery. Famous for its decoration in blue-and-white. Delftware can be plates, jugs, bowls and tiles. Fragments are a frequent foreshore find.

Denarius: An ancient Roman silver coin. They were no longer being used as the main currency during the third century—Chapter 9.

Docker: A person employed to load and unload ships—Chapter 1.

Drawdock: A sloping slipway for hauling boats out of the river. They can sometimes be used as a way to get down to the foreshore.

Earthenware: A type of pottery that is porous when fired—Chapter 10.

Ebb tide: The outgoing movement of the tide. River water levels fall, revealing the foreshore. This occurs twice daily.

Pottery found in Wapping. (*E. Vaxby*)

Eel: A fish from the Thames that can sometimes be seen washed up on the foreshore. They were once abundant in the Thames, but now the European eel population in the river has drastically declined over the last couple decades and they are now seen as a critically endangered species. Eels are very common in many traditional dishes, such as jellied eels and pies, as they were cheap and nutritious for the people in London.

Embankment: A wall built to prevent a river flooding an area. Embankments have transformed the landscape of the Thames over the centuries. There is also an Underground station called Embankment.

Equinox: The time when the sun crosses the celestial equator and when day and night are approximately equal length. This happens twice a year in spring (with the spring equinox) and in autumn (with the autumn equinox). The equinox tides often

Above: A pier-like structure in Shadwell, in between Wapping Beach and Stepney Beach. (*E. Vaxby*)

Left: A dark-blue piece of pottery. (*E. Vaxby*)

reveal stretches of foreshore that are not usually accessible, bringing new treasures to light. But these tides can also be very dangerous due to the speed and the force with which the flood tide comes in—Chapter 7.

Estuary: A partially enclosed body of water formed when two distinct bodies of water such as saltwater and freshwater mix. The Thames Estuary is the wide tidal mouth of the River Thames where it meets the North Sea. It begins at Teddington Lock and marks the transition from the flowing river to the rough sea. It has lots of mudflats and creeks along with shifting sandbanks and saltmarshes. These features make it a rich ecological landscape. There are many prehistoric archaeological discoveries that have been found closer to the sea. These are things like flint tools. It is less accessible than the central foreshore but it reminds us that the Thames is not just a famous London river, but one part of the wider history of the maritime world.

Find bag: A small bag, often plastic or dedicated to mudlarking, used for storing your finds while on the foreshore and then transporting them home. Very fragile finds will need to be wrapped up and then placed in a separate small container to protect the discovery from breaking.

Fish trap: A trap for catching fish. There are fish traps on the Thames, but they are often only accessible at low-tide. Many broken fish traps have been found on the foreshore.

Flood tide: The incoming tide, making the water levels rise. This occurs twice daily.

Flotsam: Part of a shipwreck or its cargo found floating on the sea or washed up—Chapter 1.

Flounder: A type of brackish fish living in brackish waters. It is a common fish in the Thames. A common dish with flounder in it is fried fish sandwiches.

Foreshore: The part of a shore found near the river between high and low tides. The foreshore in London is accessible in many areas but some have restrictions. Sometimes, the foreshores are muddy, with pebbles or sand—or a mixture of all three! This is the best place to mudlark. The foreshore is not only home to history, but also to many wildlife species like wading birds and crabs. Once upon a time, children played on the foreshore as if it were a coastal beach. This notably happened in the twentieth century at Tower Beach. Boats have launched from the foreshore along with people fishing here and, in the olden days, washing their clothes. The scientific name for the foreshore is the 'Intertidal Zone'. These areas suffer from erosion and accretion which can both destroy buried artifacts and reveal them to lucky mudlarks. It is often described as London's 'natural archive'—Chapter 1.

Fossil: A preserved remains or trace of an ancient organism. Fossils are at least 10,000 years old. The most common fossils found on the Thames include ammonites, crinoids, belemnites and shark teeth. These fossils may only lie centimetres away from a

The sandy foreshore in Greenwich, with the Millennium Dome seen in the distance. (*E. Vaxby*)

Victorian dinner plate, demonstrating how mudlarks have access to a pick-and-mix of treasures from through the ages—Chapter 1.

Fossil hunting: Searching for and collecting fossils. The Jurassic Coast in the south of England is famous for being a fantastic place to fossil hunt. The famous Mary Anning (21 May 1799 – 9 March 1847) fossil hunted in Lyme Regis on the Jurassic Coast. This was where she discovered the first scientifically significant plesiosaur fossil!—Chapter 1.

Garthmen: Workers at an enclosure of fish. These traps were set along the Thames to capture fish with the ebb and flow of the river. Garths are often made from stone and timber which form a funnel that fish travel through into a confined space where they could be collected easily. They used to catch fish such as eel and flounder—Chapter 1.

Georgian Era (1714–1830): The two famous writers Jane Austen and William Wordsworth were around at the time. It was begun when George I ascended the throne (following the death of Queen Anne), encompassed the Regency era, and finished when King William IV took George IV's place in 1830. The Victorian period followed.

Glaze: A glassy coating applied to pottery/ceramic for both decorative and functional purposes. There are underglazes and overglazes along with more specialised ones. Glaze comes in a variety of different colours. Some pottery patterns are known for being in one specific glaze.—Chapter 11.

Great Fire debris: The Great Fire of London burnt down thousands of buildings and a lot of the leftover materials ended up in the river. Mudlarks still recover charred timbers and melted objects from the Great Fire of 1666.

Greenwich: This part of London has both royal and naval history. It is also the centre of the world's time as the Greenwich Meridian passes through the Royal Observatory here in Greenwich. It is a prime meridian, and separates the world's time zones, with Greenwich Mean Time as the first one (+0). The National

A piece of pottery found at Stepney Beach with yellow and blue glazing. (*E. Vaxby*)

Maritime Museum also lives in Greenwich, showcasing the naval history in Greenwich, which started with the Saxons and 'Greenwic' ('wic' meant port). (Important Place Mentioned)—Chapter 1.

Halfpenny: A former pre-decimal British coin, last withdrawn in 1984. It was worth half a penny, or a 480th of a pound sterling—Chapter 1.

Heron: A tall bird frequently seen on the Thames. They hunt at low tide in shallow water, spearing fish with their sharp bills. They were hunted and eaten in medieval London.

Houseboat: A type of boat which can be moored for living in. Sometimes they are converted barges or they were built for this specific purpose—Chapter 1.

Hoy: A type of small boat with one or two masts typically used for transport. Used in medieval times up until the nineteenth century. The word 'hoy' has Dutch origins: 'hoey', meaning a small ship. With the rise of steam ships in the nineteenth century, the use of these ships gradually declined—Chapter 1.

Hydrodynamics: The study of water movement and how it affects the distribution of sediments and objects. One tide may remove layers of mud, revealing new treasures while another might bury them all again under fresh silt. Hydrodynamics impact where the best treasures are found. They can also change, altering where your favourite mudlarking spot may be.

Industrial Revolution (time period: 1760–1840): A period which brought major social and economic changes. During the Industrial Revolution there was a transition from hand production methods to machinery. Factories filled the cities, usually in harsh conditions. London was very polluted due to the burning of coal, and the Great Stink (1858) followed shortly after the Industrial Revolution. This was the time of the mudlarks! Mudlarks did not have an employer, and anyone brave enough could do it. It was a job you could easily do, if you dared! Other jobs included mining, working in a factory, working in the mills, sweeping chimneys and waste picking. Knocker-uppers were human-alarm clocks—another job if you were an early bird. Queen Victoria reigned during the latter part of the revolution. A key engineer who designed much of the infrastructure we still use today was Isambard Kingdom Brunel. He designed and built many things, such as the Great Western Railway and the SS *Great Britain*, which is now a museum ship in Bristol. His father, Marc Isambard Brunel, also helped design a tunnel under the river with Isambard Kingdom Brunel, which would later become part of the London Underground. If you would like to learn more about Brunel, visit the Brunel Museum in Rotherhithe.

In situ: A term often used for describing how you discovered a find. Photographs of an object in situ help document how you uncovered a treasure. Noting down how you found something helps give context to the find. Many of the pictures in this book were in-situ photographs.

Iridescence (glass weathering): Resembling a physical 'rainbow', showing luminous colours that appear to be different when seen

Above: A piece of blue and white coloured pottery found at Wapping Beach photographed in situ. (*E. Vaxby*)

Left: Some glass fragments with iridescence. (*E. Vaxby*)

from different angles. It is a form of glass weathering. Iridescent glass is very fragile as layers of the glass can flake off—Chapter 12.

Isle of Dogs: The Isle of Dogs is in East London, and has some good mudlarking spots. It is just across the river from Greenwich, and is not really an island. It now has residential areas, but parts of the old docks can still be seen. (Important Place Mentioned)—Chapter 5.

Jacobean Era (1603–1625): This was Shakespeare's time. King James I of England (or King James VI of Scotland) reigned during this time. The failed assassination attempt of the king (the Gunpowder Plot) happened while James was on the throne. The group who tried to blow up parliament were extreme Catholics, but Guy Fawkes and the other conspirators were caught, letting James live for another twenty years.

Jetsam: Items that are deliberately thrown into the water, perhaps for lightening the load of a ship in danger of sinking—Chapter 1.

Jetty: A small wooden or stone pier at which boats can dock or be moored. Here they could load or unload cargo. Their remains

The extremely muddy foreshore near the Isle of Dogs, London. (*E. Vaxby*)

Above: The foreshore near Canary Wharf. (*E. Vaxby*)

Below: The imprints of a bird walking on the sandy foreshore near Limehouse: a common spot to see swans and Canada geese and sometimes pigeons. (*E. Vaxby*)

(timber piles and stone footings) can still be spotted on the foreshore. They are surviving evidence of London's old port.

Kingfisher: A small, brightly coloured bird that can sometimes be spotted by the Thames. They are known for the insanitary conditions their nests are in. The colour of a kingfisher's plumage is orange and blue, making them stand out from the rest of the London crowd.

Leather: This is used in shoes, clothing and accessories (bags, belts, etc.). Leather is strong and durable but also flexible. The anaerobic mud preserves this processed animal hide well. We now also have vegan leather made from synthetic materials.

Lightermen: Workers on the river who carried goods, they lightened the ship by unloading cargo and transferred said cargo to another ship or the shore. They had boats adapted to the particular cargo they were bringing, e.g corn, stone or timber—Chapter 1.

A pipe stem with the word 'Stepney' on it, found at Wapping Beach by a fellow mudlark. (*E. Vaxby*)

Limehouse: An area in East London. Its name comes from the local lime kilns from the medieval period, though these are no longer in operation. By the eighteenth centre this part of East London had become the centre of maritime trade and shipbuilding. The Limehouse Basin opened in 1820 as the Regent's Canal Dock, which linked river traffic with the network of inland canals. From here they transported coal, timber and grain across the country. It is near Wapping and Shadwell, and has its own stop on the Docklands Light Railway service. Also home to London's first Chinatown. (Important Place Mentioned)—Chapter 1.

Limehouse Beach: Also known as Stepney Beach, this mudlarking spot is a very lucky one. It is full of oysters and pebbles, but also clay pipes and beautiful pottery and sea glass. (Important Place Mentioned)—Chapter 5.

London: The capital of England. The largest city in Great Britain. Home to some of the most diverse pages in written history—and where we mudlark on the famous River Thames! London was founded by the Romans in ad 43 with the city 'Londinium'. Roman artifacts like pottery and brooches are still regularly recovered from the foreshore. Before that there were little villages here and there. London then lived through the ages: the Black Death (fourteenth century), the Great Plague (1665–66) and the Great Fire of London (1666) all posed a threat to the city. London now has almost 9 million people! Famous landmarks include the London Eye, The Shard, the Barbican, the Tower of London and Big Ben, just to name a few—Chapter 1.

London clay: A natural geological deposit formed millions of years ago. It is under much of London and provides the foundation to the river's landscape.

Magnet fishing: A hobby where people use magnets attached to ropes to retrieve metal objects from water. It became popular in the early 2000s and since then people have uncovered all sorts of things! Magnet fishing is not permitted on the Thames—Chapter 1.

The steps to a part of the foreshore in Greenwich, viewed from below. (*E. Vaxby*)

Medieval times (time period approx. the fifth to fifteenth century): Also known as the Middle Ages, the medieval period spans a huge chunk of history. The early Middle Ages are often called the Dark Ages—the centuries that followed the fall of the Roman Empire. At this time, society was organised around the Feudal system (the monarch at the top, followed by nobles, knights, etc.).

Metal detecting: The activity where the use of metal detectors is needed to locate buried metal objects such as coins—Chapter 1.

Mooring post: Used to secure vessels during mooring. They are also known as bollards and are most commonly made from metal.

Mudflat: Broad areas of silty mud which are exposed during low-tide lying within the intertidal zone. The sediments gradually build up forming a level surface.

Mudlark: Children, poor women or elderly men who scavenged the riverbanks in the eighteenth and nineteenth centuries to find things they could sell to survive. This might include lumps of coal, rope and bits of metal. It was one of the lowest-paid and dirtiest ways to survive in London's lower class. Nowadays, it's also the name for a recreational foreshore scavenger—Chapter 1.

Mudlarking: The activity of searching the mud near rivers, famously the River Thames, for objects of value and/or interest—Chapter 1.

A plastic toy found in Greenwich, leaning against a rock on the foreshore. The river and boats on the water can be seen in the background. (*E. Vaxby*)

Two oyster shells, most likely found at Stepney Beach. (*E. Vaxby*)

Mussel: A mussel is a mollusc. They are also bivalves. Other bivalves include clams, cockles, scallops and oysters. Oyster shells are easy to spot on the foreshore due to their shiny insides.

Numismatist: A person who studies and/or collects coins and other types of currency—Chapter 14.

Nymph: A mythological spirit resembling a pretty maiden. Lives in places like woods and rivers—Chapter 10.

Oxidation layer: Also known as an oxide layer, a surface layer formed when a material reacts with oxygen. It is most commonly seen on metals and ceramics. In metals, the oxidation layer develops as corrosion products. Copper alloys develop green and brown colours, iron forms orange rust and lead may show a light grey crust. Pottery sherds might show an orangey or reddish surface formed when firing in an oxygen-rich atmosphere. The amount of patina on a metal object can help to identify the age of the item.

PAS: Portable Antiquities Scheme, for reporting treasure, see Treasure Act—Chapter 3.

Pebbles: A small, round stone made smooth by the action of water and / or sand—Chapter 2.

Above left: Some pebbles and rocks in Greenwich. (*E. Vaxby*)

Above right: A pottery shard found in Limehouse, surrounded by small smooth rocks and pebbles. (*E. Vaxby*)

Pearlware: A whiter version of creamware. It is refined earthenware pottery developed in eighteenth-century England. It was first introduced by Josiah Wedgewood around 1779 when he added a small amount of cobalt to the glaze of creamware. It has a subtle blueish tint to it, making it a better imitation of the imported Chinese porcelain—Chapter 11.

Permit: An official document giving someone authorisation to do something. The standard mudlarking permit from the Port of London Authority is needed to mudlark legally on the tidal River Thames. You can receive this permit by applying for it, though there is often a waitlist as these permits are in high demand—Chapter 1.

Pilgrim badge: These metal badges can be found on the foreshore. The wearer will have bought them at a religious site after going on a pilgrimage and worn the badge as a symbol of their personal sacrifice. The Thomas Becket Pilgrim Badge is a very common lead alloy pilgrim badge.

Pipkin: A small earthenware pot or pan with three short legs and a handle. Pipkins were very popular from the medieval period until the seventeenth century. Their legs allowed them to be set directly on a fire while the round body made boiling and stewing food easy. They often have a lead glaze inside which made them more water-tight—Chapter 10.

PLA: Port of London Authority, for foreshore maps and permits. Responsible for managing the tidal Thames. The PLA was founded in 1909 to unify the dock management systems—Chapter 1.

Porous: Minute 'holes' which air and liquid may pass through. Many ceramics are porous, like coarse earthenware fired at lower temperatures, while others are not (stoneware, which is fired at much higher temperatures, is much less porous). Unless glazed or slipped, their surfaces can absorb water and stains making them more fragile. Sherds of porous pottery often appear darker as they have absorbed minerals and organic materials from the mud and river. Stoneware survives much better than earthenware in hard conditions. Permeability is linked to porousness. Permeability is the measure of how easily a fluid can move through it. Understanding this subject can help professionals like archaeologists interpret stratigraphy (see below). Deposits with low permeability conceal the layers below them while those that are highly permeable allow salts, pollutants and sometimes even very small objects, to move between layers. This sometimes makes the dating process more difficult—Chapter 5.

Prospect of Whitby: London's oldest riverside pub, established around 1520. It is located in Wapping in the East of London and looks onto the River Thames. The Pelican stairs are on the side of

A wave crashing down onto the foreshore in Wapping just in front of the Prospect of Whitby riverside pub. (*E. Vaxby*)

the pub and lead down onto the foreshore. The pub also claims that many famous people from the past have walked through its doors, including the writers Charles Dickens and Samuel Pepys. There is a replica of a noose standing outside of the pub on the foreshore reminding everybody of where Execution Dock once lay (Important Place Mentioned)—Chapter 1.

Quay: A stone, metal or wood platform lying alongside, or projecting into, water to help with unloading and re-loading ships. In London, they were first used by the Romans—Chapter 1.

Queenhithe Dock: Meaning the queen's landing place, this historic dock is on the north bank of the River Thames, inbetween Blackfriars and London Bridge. In the medieval period this was a very busy dock and marketplace. There is now the Queenhithe Mosaic: a public artwork which celebrates 2,000 years of riverside history. This section of the foreshore is protected from mudlarks without special permission (Important Place Mentioned)—Chapter 5.

Rat: A non-native species that arrived by ship centuries ago. They love the foreshore and sometimes dead ones can be seen! Weil's disease can spread through their urine.

River: A large stream of water flowing in a channel to the sea, a lake or another river. A river starts at its source and then usually gets larger and larger as it makes its way to its mouth. The River Thames is the most famous London river and has become the centre of the mudlarking world—Chapter 1.

Riverbank: The bank of a river. Riverbanks can be man-made or natural. These boundaries are sloping and are the transition between land and water. On the River Thames, they have been shaped around the city. It is a place of work and trade.

River Brent: A tributary to the Thames: this river is almost 29km in length. That is almost 18 miles! The River Brent flows through northwest London, joining the River Thames at Brentford, a place whose name comes from 'ford on the Brent'—'ford' means a shallow place in a river allowing someone to walk across.

River Cray: This is a tributary to the River Darent (over 30km long), which then joins onto the Thames at Dartford, Kent. The River Cray's source is in Orpington which is in the London Borough of

Two pieces of red pottery with white glaze which are very similar, presumably from the same pot but broken apart on the foreshore. (*E. Vaxby*)

Bromley. In the past, St Mary Cray was a working village on the River Cray where there were mills, pubs and cottages. Roman and Anglo-Saxon artifacts have been found in the Cray River Valley.

River Effra: Now flowing underground, the River Effra had its source in Norwood Hills (near Crystal Palace) and flowed through South London. It has become part of the combined sewer system.

River Fleet: At 6km long, this river is now mostly covered but still has a rich history buried beneath the surface. It has been converted into part of the sewage system, but it used to be a place that provided the Romans with fresh water for drinking and bathing. There were also what were known as 'Fleet Marriages', which started at the Fleet Prison close to the river, where people could get married in a quick, cheap way without the whole church ceremony. The loop-hole that allowed this was tied up in 1753.

River Lea: Also sometimes called the River Lee. This river joins the Thames at Bow Creek. It starts near Luton before carving its way through Lee Valley. It is a whole 68km long! Its name is believed to have Celtic roots and the River Lea might have meant 'bright river'. By the eighteenth century it was navigable, allowing barges to carry grain timber and coal into London. Later on, they also brought gunpowder.

River Neckinger: Quite a short river that is now mostly underground but can still be seen when it flows into the Thames at St Saviours Dock. In the 1600s, convicted pirates were hanged at the wharf where this tributary entered the Thames. It is believed that the River Neckinger's name comes from the term 'devil's neckcloth', which was a slang term for the hangman's noose.

River Ravensbourne: It begins in the London Borough of Bromley and then flows for about 17km until it finally reaches the River Thames at Deptford, a foreshore famous for its maritime history. Deptford was a major naval dockyard in the past. Its foreshore is rich with shipwreck debris and lost maritime items. The likely meaning of the River Ravensbourne's name is 'boundary stream'.

Above left: A dried leaf on the foreshore in Greenwich. (*E. Vaxby*)

Above right: A small wave breaking on the foreshore in Wapping. (*E. Vaxby*)

River Roding: The River Roding is 50km long. It meets the Thames in Barking Creek near the Barking Barrier in East London. The river has a long history of flooding. The name Roding originates from 'Hroda', an Anglo-Saxon leader.

River Tyburn: Another lost river that has become part of the sewage system. Before it was converted, it was 11km (7 miles) long and rose in Hampstead and then emptied into the Thames at multiple locations near Pimlico.

River Walbrook: Now completely buried under the city, this river flowed from Shoreditch through the City of London and met the Thames near Cannon Street. Apparently, during Roman times the Walbrook divided the city Londinium into east and west parts and was lined with temples, including the famous Roman Temple of Mithras. Roman coins and amphoras made this river rich with Roman history. Flemish weaving workshops sometimes used the flow from this river in the sixteenth century.

Above left: The top of a broken wine bottle lying on the foreshore (on the north bank of the river). (*E. Vaxby*)

Above right: Lots of bones, some shells, a couple of pebbles and the bottom of a jar (on the very edge of the image), all on a sandy part of the beach by Bankside (Thames Beach). (*E. Vaxby*)

River Wandle: At 14km, this river in south London enters the Thames at Wandsworth. In the eighteenth and nineteenth centuries, the river was hard-working, powering numerous mills. The Wandle is also celebrated for having the 'greatest variety of fish'.

River Westbourne: Also called the Kilburn or the Ranelagh Sewer, the original pipe that carried it to the Thames can still be spotted at Sloane Square Underground Station in West London.

Roman Britain (time period: ad 42–410): During this time, the Romans were in charge of Britain. There was a clear division between the unconquered land in Scotland and the Roman civilisations. These two areas of land were separated by Hadrian's Wall. The culture 'Romano-British' emerged as Roman and British traditions merged. Hadrian was an emperor (he reigned from ad 117 until ad 138) who wanted to build a wall as a defence mechanism, and the wall was a symbol of Roman power. Construction on the wall began in ad 122, but it probably took around six years to build. The Romans left when their empire started to decline.

Rotherhithe: This is where the famous *Mayflower* set sail from on its way across the Atlantic. Rotherhithe is famous for its history as a port. It is in the same spot of the Thames as Limehouse, but on the South bank of the river. (Important Place Mentioned)—Chapter 1.

Sandbank: A shifting deposit affecting navigation. Forms a shallow area in the river.

Scavenge: Search for and collect anything usable from waste (discarded)—Chapter 2.

Shadwell Basin (Important Place Mentioned): FUN FACT: In the nineteenth and twentieth centuries, the majority of men in

Below left: Shadwell Basin on a cloudy day. (*E. Vaxby*)

Below right: Sherds of Willow Pattern found at different locations along the foreshore of the River Thames. (*E. Vaxby*)

Shadwell worked as seamen, watermen or in shipbuilding and repairs.

Shard: A piece of ceramic, glass, metal or rock, that is broken, typically having edges which are sharp—Chapter 10.

Shell: A shell is a protective exoskeleton of some marine animals—Chapter 5.

Sherd: Interchangeable with a 'shard' but preferred by archaeologists; a piece of broken ceramic with historical value—Chapter 11.

Slip: A liquid mixture made using clay and water—Chapter 11.

Slipware: Ceramic or pottery identified because of its decorating process where slip is placed onto leather-hard clay before firing. The slip can be dipped, painted or splashed onto the clay body—Chapter 11.

Southwark: Home to Southwark Cathedral, the London Borough of Southwark is famous for many landmarks: the Shard, Tate Modern (formerly known as the Bankside Power Station) and Shakespeare's Globe.

Three shells, found at Rotherhithe, Wapping and Limehouse. (*E. Vaxby*)

Spongeware: A type of earthenware pottery, decorated using sponges—Chapter 11.

Stoneware: A type of pottery which is impermeable and opaque (partly vitrified)—Chapter 10.

St Katherine's Dock: This dock was built in the 1800s, and takes its name from an old hospital (St Katherine's) which was founded by Queen Matilda (wife of King Stephen). The hospital is no longer there, but the dock is. It was redeveloped from the 1970s onwards and is now a lovely place you can have lunch at, or still moor a boat! (Important Place Mentioned)—Chapter 1.

Stratigraphy: The study of layers of soil, deposits and sediments (also known as strata). These layers build up over time.

Swan: These beautiful birds travel together in large families up and down the river. They are frequently spotted at Stepney Beach by Limehouse.

Tableware: Crockery, cutlery and some forms of glassware used at a table when serving and eating—Chapter 11.

A piece of white pottery with light blue stripes, found on the foreshore at Wapping Beach. (*E. Vaxby*)

Thames: Longest river in England (215 miles), navigable for 191 miles. One hundred and thirty-four bridges cross the Thames, and there are forty-four locks above Teddington. It is famous for running through London, and its daily tides (there are usually two low tides and two high tides per day). The river can be split into two parts: tidal and non-tidal. These tides are what bring our mudlarking treasures to the surface!

Thames Barrier: The retractable barrier system constructed to give protection to the floodplain of the majority of Greater London—Chapter 7.

Thames Clippers: Now known as Uber Boat by Thames Clippers, this river service was founded on 24 May 1999—Chapter 1.

Thames Frost Fairs: These Thames Frost Fairs happened during the Little Ice Age (approx. 1300 until 1850), when the Thames would freeze over. A carnival was held on top of the frozen river. There were food vendors, markets and activities like ice skating. The last official frost fair was held in 1814, which was the last time the river froze solid enough for a safe fair. There are paintings of these events which depict the lively 'city-on-ice'.

Thames River Police: The world's first river police, established in 1798—Chapter 1.

Thimble: A small cap made of metal, plastic or leather etc., with a closed end, worn to protect a sewists finger and help them push the needle—Chapter 10.

Tide: The rising and falling of the sea, usually twice each lunar day due to the attraction of the moon and sun at a particular place—Chapter 1.

Torpedo bottle: A uniquely shaped bottle designed for carbonated drinks—Chapter 12.

Tosher: A sewer scavenger often compared to mudlarks.

Tower Hamlets: A borough in London stretching across Spitalfields, Wapping, Whitechapel, Shadwell, Bethnal Green, Stepney, Limehouse, Mile End and Canary Wharf. Some of it was previously docklands.

Above: Moored boat near Wapping, with the tall Shard (a London landmark) in the background. (*E. Vaxby*)

Right: An image taken by the Isle of Dogs of a very muddy foreshore, with algae and rocks on the surface. (*E. Vaxby*)

A piece of blue and white pottery in a wing-like shape. (*E. Vaxby*)

Trade token: A coin-like object used as currency—Chapter 10.

Transferware: A type of ceramic where the pottery is decorated using a transfer printing process—Chapter 11.

Treasure Act: The Treasure Act 1996 defining the treasure that must be reported. It means that you must report potential treasure within fourteen days. It was updated in 2023 with an expansion on what was considered treasure.

Tributary: A smaller river or major stream that joins into a larger river. For example, the River Lea is a tributary to the River Thames. The River Lea is among over thirty of the other major waterways connecting to the Thames. The River Kennet is the largest joining tributary.

Trowel: A handheld tool varying in size, with a flat and pointed blade. They are often used in gardening or when spreading mortar when building—Chapter 3.

Tudor Era (1485–1603): The Tudor Era was the time when five monarchs from the House of Tudor sat on the throne. This was Henry VII, Henry VIII (famous for his six wives!), Edward VI, Mary I (often known as 'Bloody Mary') and Elizabeth I (the 'Virgin Queen'). They were succeeded by the House of Stuart. There was also Lady Jane Grey in between Edward and Mary, but she reigned for only nine days. The poor were in the majority of the population but life for them was hard.

Tudor Greenware: Used to describe thin-walled, green-glazed, white-fired earthenware produced during Tudor times. It was made in Surrey and Hampshire around the fifteenth century. These ceramics were very popular at the time and lots of fragments have been found on the foreshore—Chapter 11.

Tupperware: A brand name: a range of plastic containers used to store food—Chapter 5.

Green and clear glass (including a glass stopper) and an indigo coloured glass fragment. (*E. Vaxby*)

Verdigris: A bright green patina caused by corrosion which sometimes forms on bronze and copper when exposed to moisture. Mudlarks often uncover things like copper nails and pins, along with coins that are coated in verdigris.

Victorian Era (1837–1901): The reign of Queen Victoria, sixty-three years and 216 days. That makes her the second-longest reigning monarch in British history, second only to Queen Elizabeth II. Queen Victoria was only just 18 years old when she ascended the throne. Times were tough during the Victorian era, but many significant technological and social changes also took place. Families often had more than seven children, so earning enough money to provide for them could be a struggle. Milk maids and newsboys are included in the long list of jobs you could have as your occupation during the Victorian times. Charles Dickens was a prominent author during the Victorian period.

Waders: High boots which are waterproof, often used for fishing or when walking into a body of water—Chapter 14.

Wapping: Wapping is famous for being the site of the old Execution Dock, where traitors were hanged. A very long time ago it was a marshy land, which could have been the origin of Wapping's name. It is now a cozy corner of London, with residential warehouses, dance and theatre schools, sports teams and parks and so much more, all just a step away from the foreshore. (Important Place Mentioned)—Chapter 1.

Wapping Beach: Both a pebble and a sand beach. Located near the Prospect of Whitby. It has multiple entrances with steps. Sea glass, pipe bulbs, pottery and much more can be found here. (Important Place Mentioned)

Warehouse: A large building where materials and goods can be stored before distribution—Chapter 1.

Warehouseman: Someone who owns, manages or is employed in a warehouse. It was a common job during the industrial revolution—Chapter 1.

Waterman: A river worker transferring passengers across or along the river—Chapter 1.

A photograph of bricks near Wapping Wall, taken on the way to the foreshore. (*E. Vaxby*)

Westminster: Home to Westminster Abbey and the Houses of Parliament (and Big Ben which is the nickname for the Great Bell inside of the Elizabeth Tower), this part of London is named Westminster because the abbey was the monastery located to the west of the City of London. Lambeth is on the opposite bank. Lambeth was originally called Lambehitha, meaning the 'landing place of lambs', before being shortened to simply Lambeth.

Wharf: A level quayside area where a ship can be moored (loading and unloading)—Chapter 1.

Wherry: A type of boat traditionally used for carrying passengers and/or cargo—Chapter 1.

Whiteware: A category of ceramic products which are white and off-white in colour—Chapter 11.

Wooden pile: A wooden post that is driven vertically into the ground to support a piece of infrastructure. On the foreshore, that means being a part of a structure like a quay, revetment or jetty.

Yacht: A type of medium-sized boat ready for racing and cruising. They are sometimes spotted on the Thames or in St Katherine's Dock near Wapping—Chapter 1.

Select Bibliography

Ackroyd, Peter, *Thames: Sacred River*, (London: Penguin Books, 2008).

Hume, Ivor Noël, *Treasure in the Thames*, (London: Frederick Muller Ltd, 1956).

Maiklem, Lara, A *Mudlarking Year: Finding Treasure in Every Season*, (London: Bloomsbury, 2024)

Roberts, Greg, 'An Account of Peggy Jones, the London Mudlark', Wicked William, 29 June 2018, https://www.wickedwilliam.com/an-account-of-peggy-jones-the-london-mudlark/ (accessed 15 August 2025)

Sandy, Jason, 'Mudlarking: Ancient Pottery' *Beachcombing Magazine*, 6 October 2021, https://www.beachcombingmagazine.com/blogs/news/mudlarking-ancient-pottery (accessed 15 August 2025)

Sandy, Jason, 'Mudlarking: Bellarmine Jugs and Witch Bottles', *Beachcombing Magazine*, 10 September 2019, https://www.beachcombingmagazine.com/blogs/news/bellarmine-jugs-and-witch-bottles (accessed 15 August 2025)

Sandy, Jason, 'Mudlarking: Buttons with Backstories', *Beachcombing Magazine*, 17 January 2022, https://www.beachcombingmagazine.

Above: Two clay pipes from the collection of Corinne Gilson, gifted to me a few years ago. (*E. Vaxby*)

Below: The sun setting behind London's skyline. (*E. Vaxby*)

com/blogs/news/mudlarking-buttons-with-backstories (accessed 15 August 2025)

Sandy, Jason, 'Mudlarking: The Mystery of the Thames Garnets', *Beachcombing Magazine*, 12 July 2018, https://www.beachcombingmagazine.com/blogs/news/mudlarking-the-mystery-of-the-thames-garnets (accessed 15 August 2025)

Sandy, Jason, *MUDLARKS: Treasures from the Thames*, (California, USA: Silver Gravity Publishing, 2022)

Scott, Kirtsi, 'A Sea of Colors', *Beachcombing Magazine*, 11 October 2021, https://www.beachcombingmagazine.com/blogs/news/a-sea-of-colors-1 (accessed 15 August 2025)

Smith, Julia, 'Mudlarking on the Thames, London', Blogpost, https://mudlarking.blogspot.com/ (accessed 15 August 2025)

'The Prospect of Whitby and Shadwell Basin', *A London Inheritance*, 27 November 2016, https://alondoninheritance.com/londonpubs/the-prospect-of-whitby-and-shadwell-basin/ (accessed 15 August 2025)